A brief taste of some of the grapes covered in
Peter Hellman's
AMERICAN WINE HANDBOOK

Cabernet sauvignon
You might call cabernet the purest of all fine wine
grapes. By that, I mean that in the journey from
grape into wine, it seems to travel furthest.

Pinot noir
If cabernet sauvignon is the intellectual's wine, then
Pinot noir belongs in the glass of the sensualist. It is
a wine of a uniquely velvety texture and softness.

Fumé blanc
Crisp and herbal scented, its pleasure is its firmness,
its sprightliness, and its straightforward fresh
character.

Johannisberg Riesling
Of the great varietals, Riesling is the lightest on its
feet. It can achieve great intensity of fruity flavor
and yet not overwhelm a plainly broiled fish or the
white meat of chicken.

THE AMERICAN WINE HANDBOOK

Peter Hellman

BALLANTINE BOOKS • NEW YORK

Library of Congress Catalog Card Number: 87-91474

ISBN 0-345-33097-8

Manufactured in the United States of America

First Edition: September 1987

CONTENTS

INTRODUCTION

WHAT is this book designed to do for you?

It is meant to save you time in educating yourself to the pleasures of wine. It will do so by laying out the guidelines that need to be kept in mind as you proceed with your vinous education. Specifically, it will cover:

—what you need to know, and no more—about how the grape becomes wine and what forms wine can take.

—which wine grapes are used for what purposes.

—how to evaluate the quality and seriousness of a wine shop and how to select from its shelves.

—how to react when handed a restaurant's wine list.

—how to get more pleasure out of sparkling wines.

—when the time is right to bring out a special bottle and when that gesture will be wasted.

—what wines will make your traditional holiday meals most enjoyable.

1

—which wine it makes sense to "cellar" and which ought to be bought only when needed.

—what is the best way to open a wine bottle and which glasses will allow the wine to show its best.

Most of all, this book will offer you guidelines and intelligent options for choosing wines to enrich all the phases of what we dare to call civilized dining—wines for sipping as aperitifs, for the end of a meal, and for all that unfolds in between.

Finally, this is a book in which the emphasis is on the enjoyment of American wines on their home soil. Our wines haven't always merited that emphasis. But they certainly do now. In less than two decades, American winemakers have turned a desultory industry into one that is producing wines as fine as any on earth. And with each vintage they only get better and more various. Now we shall see how and why this new era has come so happily upon us.

A
SHORT
HISTORY
OF
AMERICAN
WINE

J U S T after midnight on December 1, 1933, in the prevailing pastoral calm of the Napa Valley, Louis M. Martini—a man who liked to raise a ruckus—unlocked the door of his winery. As required by the 18th Amendment to the Constitution, that door had been locked for fourteen years. Now, flashlight in hand, he entered the musty space and, finding the cord to the steam whistle on the winery's roof, he let loose a continuous blast that filled the valley for nearly half an hour.

That act of jubilation marked the legal end of the years called Prohibition (1919–33). As we well know, neither booze nor wine ceased to be demanded or produced in those years. Thanks to legions of moonshiners and bootleggers, it was an exceptionally gay time—but not for the formerly legitimate producers, like Martini. It was illegal for Americans not only to buy wine during Prohibition. It was illegal even to approach the premises of a winery.

The few who, like Martini, had kept the winemaker's faith in that dark age were now hoping that the way was clear to resume the making of fine wines in America. But that optimism was misplaced, or at

5

least premature. Too much damage had been done—not merely to the art and industry of winemaking but to the consumer's appreciation of the product as well. All manner of misfortune had befallen winemakers everywhere in America prior to Prohibition, and more was to come before they would flourish at last.

Our schoolbooks tell us that Leif Ericson named this continent "Vimland" on account of the profusion of grapevines he found growing on its shore. The native grapes, however, were not meant for the making of fine wine—at least not wine to please those palates accustomed to the traditional European grape varieties known as *Vitis vinifera* (literally, "wine bearer"). If Ericson really did see grapevines (some speculate it might have been look-alike squashberries), they were surely of another family, alien to Europe, called *Vitis labrusca*. Wine from *labrusca* has the "foxy" bold flavor (Concord red wine is the most familiar example) that is so striking at first smell and taste but, lacking subtlety, doesn't wear well.

The lack of finesse to wines made from native grapes was lost neither on the colonists nor on those to whom the wine was shipped back home. Numerous early attempts were made to establish vineyards using *vinifera* grape cuttings sent from Europe. But the vines inevitably sickened and died. Even expert viticulturists imported to the New World could not make them thrive. The town of New Bordeaux, South Carolina, for example, was founded in 1764 by French Huguenots who intended to make it in the image of its namesake. They had been granted thirty thousand acres by the British crown to found a grape and wine industry. Even the determined Huguenots failed.

It is said that the ever-resourceful Thomas Jefferson, whose belief in fine wine was devout, went so far as to import actual French earth to Monticello in which to make French vines feel at home. Still, they did not thrive. Conceding defeat in 1803, Jefferson wrote that it would perhaps be best to work with native grapes, whatever their deficiencies, in the hope that a way could be found to make them into fine wines. They, at least, would survive for as long as it took to make the effort.

Jefferson never knew that the unseen and undetected principal killer of *vinifera* on American soil was a mite called phylloxera, which burrowed into the roots of the vine and killed them. But it did not attack roots of native grapes. Phylloxera went undetected, remarkably, from colonial times into the second half of the nineteenth century. The little mites are said to have been (can anyone really know?) in a cargo of sample vines that were shipped to England in 1848. From there they spread to France. Feasting on *vinifera* rootstock on the home ground, phylloxera systematically killed nearly all the vineyards of France, Italy, and Germany during the second half of the nineteenth century—millions upon millions of vines.

As the curse had come from America, so did salvation. French viticultural experts discovered that shoots from *vinifera* could be grafted onto the base of louse-resistant American rootstock. Painstakingly, this surgery was carried out millions of times in both

Europe and America. Phylloxera was not finally put at bay until the beginning of this century.

The history of the wine grape in California commences with the plantings of the Spanish *padres* in the seventeenth century. The fat black grapes they used for making sacramental wines became known as "Mission" grapes. This variety had no more potential for making fine wine than did the Eastern *labrusca*. But customers in the American West were not yet so choosy. By 1835, several commercial growers had taken hold in the budding little city of Los Angeles. The biggest of these vineyards, owned by one Juan de Sera, was on land currently occupied by the city's railroad station.

By the middle of the nineteenth century, after two centuries of effort, America had yet to produce wines to boast about. But the second half of the century would change that situation much for the better. In the East, improvement came as viticulturists experimented with thousands of strains of native grapes to identify and cultivate those that performed best. The emerging stars of this array were the Catawba, introduced in 1823 by Major John Adlum in Washington, D.C., and the Concord, developed by Ephraim Bull in its namesake Massachusetts village. (The spot was just across the way from Nathanial Hawthorne's cottage.) In Cincinnati, meanwhile, the underpinnings of America's first great "champagne" enterprise were being established by the New York–born entrepreneur Nicholas Longworth. By 1858, his "Sparkling Catawba" was of such repute that it was actually exported to England.

The California wine world at mid-century was dominated by a single dramatic figure—the black-eyed, hyperactive "Count" Agoston Haraszthy. He had been exiled by the monarchy from his native Hungary in 1840, apparently, for being one blueblood who was too sympathetic to the call for a revolution among the common folk. After a six-year stopover in Wisconsin, where the grapevines he planted did not survive the harsh winters, he headed to California in 1846. Eleven years later, after a thorough search for the ideal vineyard site in the state, he established the magnificent Buena Vista wine estate in Sonoma, complete with Pompeiian villa. Two of Haraszthy's sons married, in a double ceremony, daughters of his neighbor General Mariano Vallejo, who had the distinction of being the last Spanish governor of what had been the colony of California. Haraszthy was a model of the progressive viticulturist, promoting the best *vinifera* grapes rather than the plump but common Mission variety.

In 1861, Haraszthy traveled to Europe on behalf of the governor of California to collect grape cuttings that might thrive in the state. He did his job well, returning with an astonishing 200,000 cuttings. By then, Buena Vista was California's largest winery. Haraszthy "took it public" as the Buena Vista Horticultural Society. It was not a moneymaker, and by 1866 Haraszthy had hurriedly departed for Nicaragua. The story goes that he met his end there by drowning or by being eaten by crocodiles, or both.

Buena Vista's days of glory and glamour had so totally been forgotten that when the 450-acre estate was put up for auction in 1941, nobody seemed to know of its remarkable builder. And so it would have remained if the new owner, Frank Bartholomew, had not become curious about some stone ruins on the property. He called in the premier American wine historian Leon Adams, who identified the remains as a part of Haraszthy's Buena Vista.

The long and difficult apprenticeship of American winemaking had finally been completed with the arrival of the boom years that followed the Civil War. New York, Ohio, and California were the leaders in offering a full range of still, sparkling, and fortified wines on the European model. Great names in American wine that would survive to this day were established. In California, they included Inglenook, Beringer, Simi, Paul Masson, Krug, and Beaulieu. In New York, the most noteworthy were Great Western and Gold Seal—both specialists in sparkling wine. At the Paris Exposition of 1889, California's Cresta Blanca Vineyards won two gold medals for white wine. At the 1900 Exposition, American wines took a startling total of thirty medals. While California did best, the breadth of the country's serious winemaking effort was demonstrated by winning wines from Florida, North Carolina, Virginia, and even Washington, D.C.

The new century ought to have begun with limitless expectations for American wine. So much had been learned, and the dread phylloxera had been beaten. But a political disaster was now in the making. Maine had gone dry in 1851, and "as Maine went, so went the nation." Kansas, home of Carrie Nation, went dry in 1880. Iowa was next, in 1883. In

1893, an Ohioan named Frances Willard amalgamated the numerous temperance societies of the nation into the Anti-Saloon League. She would claim that in a period of six years, not a day went by when she failed to give at least one speech against the evils of alcohol.

Table wine was only a minor culprit in the array of bottles on the saloon shelf. Certainly, it was not the primary destroyer of the drinker and his or her family. Hard liquor, which could contain quadruple the alcohol of wine, was to blame for that. But wine was swept up too in the Prohibitionist fervor. Even the Bible's numerous affirmative references to wine were of no avail. Psalm 103, for example, tells us that "wine gladdens the heart of Man." Scholarly texts appeared arguing that what the psalmist actually referred to was the juice of the grape *before* it was fermented.

The Congress enacted the 18th Amendment to the Constitution on December 18, 1917. It was quickly ratified by every state except two (Rhode Island and Connecticut). In January 1919, America became an entire land where beverages containing more than one half of one percent of alcohol were illegal. But the fine print loomed large. Wines for sacramental, medicinal, and industrial purposes were authorized. Families could vinify up to two hundred gallons of "juice" wine annually, which comes to an astonishing total of a thousand normal bottles! This liberality was meant to pacify the apple growers' lobby, much of whose product had traditionally been allowed to ferment into "hard" cider. But it was the winegrowers who leaped into the hole in the law.

Paradoxically, the demand for grapes intensified during the first years of Prohibition—especially in the great cities where the message of the "dries" wasn't so much appreciated as in small towns and the farmlands. In the harvest season, entire sections of urban railyards had to be set aside for hectic commerce in grapes arriving from California.

With such demand for grapes from home winemakers, it might have seemed that the finest vineyards were in no danger from Prohibition. But that was not the case. Fine wine grapes were beautiful primarily to the winemaker, who knew how they would be magically transformed by vinification. To a shipper, however, they were too perishable for the cross-country trip. To a shopper, these grapes tended to be thick-skinned and puckery to the taste. Much more appealing to the eye and taste were the plump, dark red Alicante-Bouschet, a mediocre wine grape, or, better yet, the Thompson Seedless, a table grape. (By contrast, the Chardonnay grape, from which the finest white wine on earth is made, is a tart, underflavored, and generally unappealing munching grape.)

It takes years for a new vineyard of fine wine grapes to come to maturity. As the vines grow thick and gnarly their yield diminishes, but the character of the grapes they do produce grows more intense. Forty-year-old vines are the pride of a vintner. But it was just such vines that were ripped out of California vineyards during Prohibition in favor of varieties that were high-yielding, delicious, and beckoning to the shopper. The truth was that few families kept up an interest in fine wine, anyway. Perhaps the worst legacy of Prohibition was that it didn't destroy the American taste for "booze"—only for alcohol in its noblest manifestation: well-crafted wine.

The cracking of the midnight air by Louis Martini's whistle that December midnight in 1933 meant that American vineyards could be replanted, that equipment in disrepair could be restored, and that the men skilled in fine winemaking, now scattered, could be called back to the wineries. Restoring the fine wine standard that had been destroyed over fourteen years, however, was not so easy. This standard must be upheld by both producer and consumer; it is the mutual insistence on such a standard that is responsible for the superb quality of restaurants in France, for example. It isn't something that can be legislated. It is carried in the heads and hearts of those who honor it.

What Americans carried around mainly, in those post-Prohibition years, was an ongoing predilection, if not a downright lust, for booze. Their feeling toward wine was, at best, tolerant, as long as it was on the sweet side. Before Prohibition, two-thirds of domestic wine production had been dry. Afterward, two-thirds of it consisted of American "sauternes," dessert sherries, and other sweet wines. Those labels that today proudly carry *vinifera* names—Cabernet Sauvignon, Chardonnay, Pinot Noir, Sauvignon Blanc—would have spelled commercial disaster for any winery foolish enough to attempt to sell them.

For decade upon decade following Repeal, it was a

great time in America for Scotch, bourbon, gin, and vodka. It was an excruciating time for the wallflower called fine wine.

FINE WINES REBORN

It may well have been inevitable that Americans would one day rediscover a taste for fine wines. I believe that eventuality was hastened, however, by the seemingly unrelated introduction into commercial service of the large jet airplane. Beginning in the mid-1960s, Boeing 707's, with a capacity of about one hundred sixty, began carrying tourists to Europe on an ever-larger scale. It wasn't only the very wealthy or very bohemian who were going off on these vacations, as had been the case between the World Wars. Now it was the middle class. Whether in Rome, Paris, Brussels, or a simple country inn, the food they were served was, for many of them, a revelation. They had never eaten so well or so variously. And with their lunches and dinners came wine by the bottle and the carafe. That, too, was a revelation. It added the equivalent of a third dimension to what had been two-dimensional eating. Without wine, a respectable European meal simply was not complete. Why not in America?

In those years the most common beverages at any American family meal except breakfast were, in approximate order of preference: soda, milk, water, and iced tea. These liquids may not have done a great deal to complement the food they accompanied, but frankly, they weren't a single step ahead or above the prevailing culinary standard of the day.

I keep trying to remember what exactly we ate as I grew up in the fifties. Here is what was on the dinner plate in my home: hamburgers, pork chops, steak (sirloin or chuck), Swiss steak, roast or fried chicken, an occasional lamb chop or piece of fish—and enormous numbers of hot dogs. Spaghetti came in heaps with bright orange meat sauce—sometimes homemade, more often from Chef Boyardee. (The final touch of authenticity came in the shape of a green tubular container of Kraft pre-grated Parmesan cheese.)

The vegetable array on our table featured mashed or baked potatoes, green beans, peas, and succotash. In the salad bowl was Iceberg lettuce dressed with vinegar and oil or "French" dressing as bright orange as the spaghetti sauce. Bread was uniformly white and cottony—usually in square slices but sometimes in the shape of hamburger rolls. For dessert, we had Jell-O, possibly mixed with canned fruit, chocolate pudding, baked apple, and, when we were fortunate, my mother's tollhouse cookies, her ineffable blackberry pie in August, and apple pie through the autumn.

Almost nothing that I have mentioned above could be called bad food. I liked it all. It's the same food, on the whole, that I eat today. What has changed is the standard of preparation and the small details that transform a particular dish into something more pleasing to eye and palate. Why, for example, did we never think of slipping a few leaves of fresh tarragon under the skin of the chicken that was about to be roasted? Instead of boiling those fresh green beans to the deathly gray-green pallor of seasickness, why didn't we first blanch them to preserve their bright emerald color achieved at first boil and then sauté them in a touch of garlicky butter before, at the last instant, sprinkling on a handful of parsley or dill?

Why, in the salad bowl, only bland Iceberg lettuce instead of a melange of buttery Boston, spicy watercress or arugala, and, for a touch of contrasting color, one of those lovely lettuces that feather off at the edges to a red as brilliant as that of Chinese lacquer? Vinegar and oil remains the classic dressing. Why did it take us so long to discover full-flavored olive oil, or hazelnut or walnut oil? And what about deeply flavored vinegars like the Modena's balsamic or Xeres' sherry types—so mellow that you can pleasurably drink them from a spoon? Where were the unprocessed cheeses of character (not excluding those from the goat) and the breads with flavor and texture? (Yes, I know the range of available foods was narrower then—but no more so than the culinary imagination of most of the public.)

This catalog of how and what we didn't eat corresponds, of course, to a catalog of the wines we didn't drink. Wine doesn't exist in a vacuum. In order to show its noble or even its ordinary best, it needs the right food the way a dog needs love. Back then, that food wasn't available because the requisite standard didn't exist. It wasn't only in places like my hometown of Falls Church, Virginia, that it didn't exist. The situation was no different, apparently, in the heart of the wine country itself. The *Wine Institute Cookbook*, published in San Francisco in 1964, contains a compilation of recipes by winemaking families that is, by our current standard, embarrassing in its lack of imagination and its eager embrace of canned and other prepared foods. Yet it was, and is, the palate of the winemaker that determines the quality and style of the wine. Why should it have been surprising, then, if the character of the wine went right along with that of a "gourmet" main course in which the critical ingredients were ground beef plus one can each of cream of mushroom soup and cream of celery soup?

It was another cookbook from that era, ironically, that along with the aforementioned Boeing 707 turned out to be a critical tool in the revamping of American ideas about the dinner table. That book was Julia Child's *Mastering the Art of French Cooking*, first published in 1961. It had been preceded by other cookbooks devoted to the same subject, but none was so painstakingly detailed and yet so accessible to un-initiated Americans. The success of that cookbook had to be a two-way street. Julia had written it, Knopf had published it, but it was up to Americans to buy it. And buy it they did. Despite a rather stiff original price of twelve dollars (at a time when paperback books still cost as little as fifty cents), *Mastering the Art of French Cooking* had gone through eight print-ings by the end of its first decade. Now in its twenty-fourth printing, it has been joined by a companion volume and a paperback edition. Astonishingly, Julia also became the greatest star that public television has ever produced.

As Americans returned from those first tours of Europe, the more adventurous among them were de-termined to duplicate a particular dish that had been a revelation to them. *Mastering the Art of French Cooking* was their natural starting point. For the first time, Woolworth's began to get requests for wire whips and larding pins, supermarkets for fresh tarragon, shallots, and fennel bulbs, butchers for butterflied legs of lamb, duck, and sweetbreads.

After an entire Saturday devoted to marketing and cooking (how that expensive cookbook did get spattered!), it was only natural that Americans bitten by the "gourmet" food bug would also demand a new standard of wine to match their new standard of dining. What was the point of going to all the trouble to make and then triumphantly serve, say, Julia's feathery light fish quenelles or her rich and powerfully flavored beef bourguignon and then splashing an indifferent wine into the glass? At first, it was fine French wines that jumped into the breach. It was only a matter of time, however, before the American wines industry would rise to the challenge.

Until the early 1960s, California's wine country was a sleepy place. It produced more sweet wines than dry, more fortified wines than table varieties. But major progress was now occurring in the sphere of low-priced wines. Led by Ernest and Julio Gallo and advised by the wine research facility at the Davis campus of the University of California, the industry had begun to produce, in the best tradition of "building a better mousetrap," inexpensive table wines to a higher standard than any in the world. It was in the premium class that American wine had, so far, shown no inclination to excel.

The names of the French winemaking pioneers of

centuries ago are for the most part lost, but not those of the few visionaries who started the slow American march toward world-class wines. The exemplary figure of those times was, in the best American tradition, not even native-born. He was André Tchelistcheff—born in Russia and trained as a winemaker on the French Côte d'Or. Arriving in the Napa Valley in 1940, he was soon making superb Cabernet Sauvignon for Beaulieu Vineyards. Aged in small oak barrels in the French style, these wines had the texture and refinement of fine Bordeaux allied to the intensive fruitiness that was a Napa trademark.

Today, what Tchelistcheff did hardly seems remarkable. But at that time the available dry red wines were generically labeled blends like "burgundy" and "claret." Any wood aging was normally done in large redwood vats rather than in small oak barrels. The barest few wines were actually labeled Cabernet Sauvignon. In 1966, Tchelistcheff began holding aside the very best portion of Cabernet from selected vineyards, gave it extra aging, and labeled it BV "Private Reserve." Those bottlings set the most constant standard of excellence of any American red wine. A few other wineries, all in the Napa Valley, had also kept the faith in the fifties and even before: Inglenook put a "cask" number on its best Cabernets. Louis Martini used the "Special Selection" designation. Charles Krug (where the Mondavis still toiled as one family before Robert's departure in 1964 to start his own winery) put a red stripe on its "Vintage Selection" cabernets. After twenty years or more in bottle, many of these wines are still going strong. And while collectors will pay high prices for them now, wines like the

BV Private Reserve once went begging at release prices of as little as three dollars. (The magnificently suave and concentrated 1970 Private Reserve, released at $3.49, now fetches about eighty dollars.)

The situation with America's premier white wine grape, Chardonnay, was even less developed as the 1960s approached. At the time, no more than two hundred acres of this low-yielding grape were planted in California. (The most marketable white wine of the day was labeled "sauterne.") As time would prove, California Chardonnay had the potential to be as good as the most vaunted white burgundy. What it lacked in those days was the extra dimension of flavor, as well as the backbone that the canny Burgundians had long ago discovered was imparted by aging the wine in small oak barrels.

The first winery to give the blessing of real French oak to American Chardonnay was tiny Hanzell in Sonoma County. Its owner, paper magnate James D. Zellerbach, first imported French barrels when the winery opened in 1957. (To make his Burgundian point of view perfectly clear, Zellerbach built his winery in the image of the castle of Clos de Vougeot, which stands amid one of the most splendid vineyards of the Côte d'Or.) Two other California wineries that pioneered in producing Burgundian-style Chardonnay were Stony Hill and Chalone. Small production and high prices kept these wines from reaching anything close to general distribution. But they did set an example for other alert and ambitious winemakers who tasted what California Chardonnay could become.

By the mid-1970s, dozens of top-flight Chardonnays, Cabernet Sauvignons, and other varietals issued from California. The problem was that most Americans didn't yet know what strides of quality were being made—including even those who were devoted to fine wine. They still thought that wine of noble quality could come only from French soil. This prejudice was especially strong on the East Coast, which is nearly as close to Bordeaux as to Napa. Ironically, the event that caused Americans to first take notice of wines from their own soil occurred in, of all places, Paris.

It was in May 1976 that a blind tasting of top French and American Cabernet Sauvignons and Chardonnay was sponsored by Steven Spurrier, an enterprising wine merchant whose shop was located off the chic Place de la Madeleine. It was assumed that the august French entries would be shoo-ins. But the winners came instead—*quelle horreur*—from the Napa Valley. The best Cabernet was Stag's Leap Wine Cellars 1973, while Chateau Montelena's 1973 took the title among the Chardonnays. These upstarts, which had "vanquished" names as ancient and as famous as Lafite and Corton-Charlemagne, had been made by wineries that, astonishingly, were each only a year old. And far from being famous on their own side of the Atlantic, they were unknown to all but the tiniest, if not downright microscopic, coterie that was the advance guard of California wine buffs.

The results of that 1976 Paris competition made news in the press worldwide. It was obviously a stunning upset for the great French wines. And yet the wisest among America's most fervent supporters were aware that the results of a wine competition are not nearly so definitive as those of a horse race. Even championship wines are not bred to strain every muscle to "win" against slower competitors. The contents of the bottle hover somewhere between pure commodity and pure art; wine needs a proper context and full maturity to show its best. The ravishing, full-surging fruitiness of California wines did not share the context of the French wines, with their great reserve, subtlety, and even severity.

Supporters of the French red wines bided their time after the 1976 Paris competition. They assumed that, in a decade's time, the American wines would be no more than fading beauties while their own wines would just be coming into their fullest glow of maturity. That premise was tested in 1986, when the same wines were retasted in Manhattan. To the dismay of the Francophiles, the final result remained the same: The American wines were still on top. They can no longer be dismissed as "flashes in the pan." (My own feeling is that, taken on their own, the vanquished Bordeaux are as satisfying as ever. They just need their own space.)

It is universally thought that in matters of the table, the French are snobs. The truth is that they are quite open to anything edible or quaffable that is of superior quality or invention. And they do keep their ear to the ground. As early as 1974, for example, Christian Millau, co-founder of the French food and wine magazine *Gault-Millau* had already journeyed out to the wilds of California to survey the budding wine scene. His report, published in the *Gault Millau* issue of that April, was titled, "The Wines of California: A Bomb in the Cellar." It included these prophetic words: "I dare to affirm that Americans can produce not only good wines, but also very, very great wines."

It was in the early 1970s that wineries began to multiply in Napa and Sonoma counties. Most were tiny, and their founders nearly all came from professions remote from winemaking. Warren Winnarski, of Stag's Leap, had been a professor of political science. Joseph Phelps, of Phelps Winery, was a building contractor. David Bruce is still a practicing ophthalmologist. Tom Burgess was an airline pilot. Jordan Winery was founded by a man who made his fortune as an oil geologist in Indonesia. The enduring comedy team of Tom and Dick Smothers owns a winery. Jerry Seps walked out on a tenured university professorship (specializing in twentieth-century Chinese history) to found the Napa Zinfandel vineyard Storybook Mountain. Patrick Campbell of the superb little Laurel Glenn winery earned a masters degree at Harvard Divinity School and played the viola professionally before committing himself to the vine. Alex Hargrave, who with his wife, Louisa, started the first winery on the north fork of Long Island in 1973, had recently earned a master's degree in Chinese. The list goes on.

The vinous promise of California has not remained uncoveted even from abroad. Moet Hennessy, the distinguished French champagne and brandy firm, established the sparkling-wine house of Domaine Chandon in 1973. Piper Hiedeseck, in partnership with Sonoma vineyards, began Piper-Sonoma in

1978. Perhaps the most publicized bow to California's promise occurred in 1979, when Baron Philippe de Rothschild, owner of Chateau Mouton-Rothschild, entered into a winemaking partnership with the "baron" of the Napa Valley, the proud, demanding, and devoted Robert Mondavi. Their wine is called Opus One. At a price of about forty-five dollars per bottle, it is at least as expensive as Mouton-Rothschild itself.

The other great Rothschild property, Lafite Rothschild, had already paid its respects to California back in 1972. In that year, a young Frenchman named Bernard Portet became co-owner and winemaker of the little Napa winery called Clos du Val. Portet had grown up on the grounds of Chateau Lafite Rothschild, where his father had been *regisseur* (manager).

The new wave of American winemaking in the 1970s had been centered in California. But pioneers were increasingly at work elsewhere. In the Pacific Northwest, dozens of wineries sprang up. Those in the cool climes of Oregon found that they could produce wines from the difficult Pinot Noir at least as well if not better than California. These wines offered hints of the delicate yet teasingly voluptuous style that is the ideal, albeit infrequently realized, of French Burgundy itself. (This was proven, once again in Paris, in another Gault Millau blind tasting at which an Eyrie Vineyards, Oregon, Pinot Noir knocked off the great names of the Côte d'Or.)

Washington has not been quite so successful with Pinot Noir as Oregon. But it has shown itself gifted at light-bodied yet intense white wines like Sauvignon Blanc, Gewürztraminer, and Riesling. Other lovely whites have come from Idaho. A spate of new wineries have also appeared in Texas, where the winters are moderate enough to allow survival of *vinifera* grapes. Spunky little wineries have sprung up, too, in nearly all the coastal Atlantic States—notably Virginia, Maryland, New Jersey, New York, Connecticut, Massachusetts, and Rhode Island. Some of these have been true to *vinifera*. Others have concentrated on the sturdier Franco-American hybrids. Baco Noir and Chancellor are the leading red hybrids, Seyval Blanc, and Vidal the leading whites. None of these hybrids have yet made wines that have convinced anyone to desert *vinifera*. But that day may yet come.

In purely economic terms, anyone who has dared to take the plunge into developing a winery in America is committing an act of folly. Few businesses require so great an input of cash and time with so little likelihood of eventual profit. Young vines don't produce fruit for at least three years. Winery equipment is fearfully expensive. A modern press, for example, can cost at least $12,000, a bottling line $20,000. New French oak fifty-gallon barrels currently cost $275. Even a relatively small winery will need at least a hundred barrels. With red wines, at least two years will pass from the vintage date until the wine can be marketed. The best Chardonnays, too, need time in oak.

Once the bottled wine is ready to leave the winery, it must scrap its way onto retail wine shelves that are already overcrowded with wines from around the world. Lacking a track record, however, a first wine is like a first novel. The public rarely takes notice. Consumers are creatures of habit. They know what has pleased them in the past. Why gamble on a new label? Gaining recognition, and then brand loyalty, is a process that tests the finances and the spirit of a young winery. And yet it is done over and over again. In the decade beginning in 1970, the number of California wineries increased from 366 to 794. In the Atlantic coastal states, the total jumped from 28 to 92. Nationwide, the number of farms decreases as the number of wineries increases. There were 1,240 wineries active in 1985. Fewer than half of them had existed prior to 1975.

And why do they do it, these men and women who plunge into the winery business? Why leave secure and lucrative professions for an enterprise with a poor prognosis for survival, let alone success? They do it for the same reason that restless spirits once cast aside all that they could count on to set out to write the great American novel. It was the challenge of producing something highly personal and artful. The winemaker, however, has one highly unfair, perhaps even unjust, advantage over the novelist: The bottle is more often finished than the book.

NAMING
NAMES

THE RED WINE GRAPES

CABERNET SAUVIGNON

Character

Of all fine wine grapes, you might call Cabernet the purest. By that I mean that in the journey from grape into wine, it seems to travel furthest. Other red wines, like Gamay or Zinfandel, give off the direct scent of their grape in their youth, but young Cabernet Sauvignon has an abstract quality. It is a wine of backbone rather than prettiness. You will hear attributed to Cabernet a spectrum of scents and tastes— cedar, mint, mushrooms, damp leaves, leather, cassis. And they might all be there together in one wine. That is because Cabernet Sauvignon, more than any other wine, has its flavors in layers. In the best Cabernets, these layers peel back for you, one after the other. As soon as one insinuates itself into your senses, as in pattern of rich shadow that is never still, up comes another. This layering of scent and flavor is what wine writers call, for lack of a more adequate word, "complexity." It is an inner dance of flavors.

If you doubt the distance that Cabernet Sauvignon travels in becoming wine, ask a vineyardist to let you taste the ripe grape at harvest time. It will be a runty, thick-skinned specimen that will make your mouth pucker. It has none of the qualities that it gives to wine. (A fine eating grape like Thompson Seedless, on the other hand, is all abrim with sweet flavor but makes an insipid wine.)

The French Framework

In 1855, the wine brokers of Bordeaux established a still-standing classification of 56 of the best chateaus in the Médoc—the bleak peninsula to the northwest of the city. (The brokers also included Chateau Haut-Brion, a property so famous it couldn't be ignored, even though it is in the Graves district, south of Bordeaux, rather than in the Médoc.) The wines are divided into five classes according to quality. They vary widely in style, and each has its particular personality. What they all have in common, however, is that their chief constituent is the Cabernet Sauvignon grape. With due consideration to other glorious wines of France, these wines of the Médoc are the favorite of more people worldwide than any others.

In its youth Cabernet Sauvignon is a nasty wine nearly everywhere it is made. But it is nastiest of all on its home turf in the Médoc. Even the French, who have a higher tolerance than we Americans for wines that are ungratefully sharp in youth, shrink back from drinking Cabernet Sauvignon straight. So it is almost always blended with grapes that soften and round it out—Merlot and Cabernet Franc, mainly. At chateaus where little or no blending is done—Mouton-Rothschild is the outstanding example—the wine is many years slower in reaching fullest drinkability than are most other fine wines of the Médoc.

In America

Cabernet Sauvignon is the undisputed prince among American red wines. No other grape is planted by so many wineries. No other red wine fetches such high prices. American Cabernet Sauvignon tends to be softer, fruitier, riper, even lusher, than the French model. But it is still a wine where the backbone and sternness show through. And despite very different growing conditions, our Cabernet Sauvignon also retains that remarkable individuality of the chateau wines. The good bottles have a way of sticking in your mind the way no other wine does.

Cabernet Sauvignon produces notable wines almost everywhere it is planted in America. Napa Valley wineries were the first to excel. But Sonoma County now produces at least as many fine examples. To the north, Mendocino County has its share of lighter-style versions. Below San Francisco, the wineries of Santa Cruz, Monterey, San Luis Obispo, and Santa Barbara counties (known collectively as the "Central Coast") are much newer at Cabernet Sauvignon production.

Not long ago, the discussion of "serious" Cabernet Sauvignon would have ranged up and down California—but no further. Today, intriguing and impressive examples are being made in the Pacific Northwest, in Texas, and, most promising of all, in the Middle Atlantic States. These wines rarely if ever have the weight of their West Coast brethren. At first, they also lacked the concentration of flavor and sense of style to put them in the same class. But as vines and wine-making techniques mature year by year, these wines get ever better. Byrd Vineyards, in the Cactoctin foothills of Maryland, has been a standout even in competition with a full range of California heavyweights. These East Coast wines have echoes of French style. In an age that plays down the un-French muscle of so many California wines, this will work in their favor.

Uses

Those who take most naturally to drinking Cabernet Sauvignon on its own are Englishmen dressed in well-cut tweed suits—or so it seems to me on those limited occasions when I am in a London wine bar. They can often be seen after work in these cozy places, seated in pairs at small round tables, putting away a bottle of claret (the traditional English term for red Bordeaux) between them as they chat. This normally wiles away a civilized forty minutes, after which they may well order another bottle—still without a morsel in sight. Americans would get a little drunk and quite starved by this ritual, but it seems not to affect Englishmen.

Cabernet Sauvignon wants food just as food wants *it*. Which foods? Lamb is the classic match for the very best bottles. A veal chop or roast also makes a nice match, so long as the wine is on the subtle side. That style will also suit a roast chicken. The richer versions will perform well with beef or the gamier birds and with cow's milk cheeses that aren't too strong. The larger strategy is to use more incisive and intense examples of Cabernet Sauvignon to cut through richly textured foods. Lighter examples match less opulent foods.

MERLOT
Character

You might think of Merlot as a slightly unfocused variation on Cabernet Sauvignon—blurred at the edges in both taste and texture. A young "cab" can be lean, stern, tough. It will bite your gums with tannin. Merlot is more likely to be rounder, softer, gentler in the mouth. The "mouth feel" can seem to be almost fuzzy. The taste of young American Merlot often suggests cherries. As with Cabernet Sauvignon, however, it is hard to put a finger on what Merlot tastes like once it matures—which is not a criticism. Most of all, you'll find yourself coming back to those soft edges. Merlot gives the impression of looking through the lens of a camera that isn't quite in focus—only, since the image I have in mind is of flowers, the effect is exceedingly pleasant.

The French Framework

It's that gentleness which has made Merlot the grape most depended on to blend with and soften the rock-hard Cabernet Sauvignon grapes of the Médoc. Some clarets are as much as fifty-percent Merlot. Inland from Bordeaux, in the communes of Saint-Emilion and Pomerol, Merlot succeeds Cabernet

Sauvignon as the principal grape. It reaches its fullest glory at tiny Chateau Pétrus, where the wine is normally 100 percent Merlot—a wine remarkable for its lush, even plush, texture. Pétrus is currently the most expensive wine of Bordeaux. The 1982 vintage was selling, in the year of its release (1985) for a staggering and, frankly, preposterous $2,000 per case. This makes the Merlot vines of Pétrus the most precious of any in the world.

In America

Until quite recently, Merlot hardly existed in America. As of 1960, none was planted in California. The lack of interest in the grape corollated to a lack of need for a softening agent for the state's Cabernet Sauvignon. With its round and fruity character, California "cab" was approachable in its pure form. California vintners were proud to offer a 100-percent Cabernet that could be sipped at a relatively early age. It was Louis M. Martini who, in the late 1960s, first began to grow Merlot in order to see if it would add interest to his Napa Valley Cabernets. The results of Martini's blending experiment, like those of most wine experiments, aren't conclusive. What is certain, however, is that his pure Merlot has turned out to be an extraordinarily graceful wine. And that grace doesn't imply blandness.

The last ten years have seen a rising interest in Merlot for its own sake. Acreage in California had grown by 1980 to 2,400 acres. Merlot has become a wine of pride for medium-size wineries like Sterling, Rutherford Hill, Stag's Leap Wine Cellars, and Clos du Bois. And it has become a grape that has caught the attention of a number of young new wineries determined to make names for themselves. The biggest splash has been made by Napa's Duckhorn, which may be the first winery to get top dollar for its "Tres Palmas" Merlot ($18) rather than for its best Cabernet Sauvignon ($14). This kind of a wine is a departure from the affable, gentle-natured Merlots in the Martini style. Though not lacking a certain plushness that is typical of the grape, they share with the French Pomerols a sense that they have real bones as well as flesh.

As the star of 100-percent Merlot wines has risen, that of 100-percent Cabernet Sauvignon has fallen. It is no longer considered *declassé* or un-Californian to blend other grapes with Cabernet Sauvignon in the French way. It can make a more interesting wine on these shores as well as those of the Médoc. This is done across the board, from the moderately priced BV "Beautour" Cabernet (about $6), which usually includes about 15-percent Merlot, to the expensive Phelps "Insignia" (about $25), which in certain years is fully 50-percent Merlot. The proper blending of Cabernet Sauvignon, Merlot, and perhaps a dollop of Cabernet Franc is a key to the shift that so many California wineries are now intent on—from sheer power to elegance. The more considerate among these wineries will list the percentage of each grape on the label—something that French wineries never do.

Since federal regulations require that a wine must be at least 75 percent of a particular grape to merit that name on the label, the makers of the most "democratic" blends are in a bind when it comes to naming their wines. Some wineries, like Parducci and Hargrave, have put the unwieldy term "Cabernet-Merlot" on the label. Others have selected a trade name for their blends, like the Joseph Phelps "Insignia" and Clos du Bois Marlestone (the vineyard name). The conscientious new Lyeth winery simply calls its blend "Red Table Wine," a term previously reserved for wine that is much less expensive. And the most prestigious of all—the joint venture of Robert Mondavi and Baron Philippe de Rothschild—is marketed as "Opus One." These are all very expensive wines—more so than most bottles of straight Cabernet Sauvignon.

Uses

No dish that I know of cries out for Merlot above all other wines as its perfect partner. That's because it is a wine that usually lacks a forcefully pointed personality of its own. Cabernet Sauvignon is harder, Pinot Noir is softer, and Merlot hovers in between. I'd serve it with roast beef, which seems to want a more rounded flavor than Cabernet normally provides. Merlot is also a fine drink with any kind of meat stew. With many components in the pot, the stew doesn't need a more incisive wine. Don't hesitate to serve Merlot as a stand-in for Burgundy, as with the more intensely flavored birds like duck or goose.

PINOT NOIR
Character

If Cabernet Sauvignon is the intellectual's wine, then Pinot Noir belongs in the glass of the sensualist. It is, ideally, a wine of uniquely velvety texture and soft contours. The wine writer Peter Quimme has aptly used the word "bosomy." Though vinified as totally dry as any table wine, Pinot Noir can have a haunting sweetness. Among the red wine grapes, it is the lightest in color. Some examples look positively feeble as they get older. You would be pardoned for mistaking them for a rosé rather than a red. But don't be fooled. That pale wine is capable of delivering billows of flavor, gentle but firm, that can last long after you have swallowed.

The French Framework

The home ground of Pinot Noir is a low, east-facing hillside that stretches for some seven miles above and below the Burgundian city of Beaune at the center of France. It is called the Côte d'Or (Slope of Gold), and, notwithstanding the meagerness of the soil, no name ever seemed more fitting. Its wines are, at their best, inimitably beguiling. But like so much else that is beguiling, they are inconstant. The problem is that Pinot Noir is the most finicky of the great red grapes. Instead of the ethereal quality of which they are capable, Burgundian reds too often can seem merely washed-out. This seems to be the case more frequently now than in decades past. And it has happened at a time when the prices of Burgundian wines have never been higher.

In America

As was pointed out above, Pinot Noir is the most inconstant of grapes—and never more so than in America. It is the one grape that has most stubbornly resisted the efforts of American winemakers determined to recreate that Burgundian magic. Too often it will make a perfectly pleasant, or even impressive, wine, but not one that will smooth out to the velvetiness, the ineffable delicacy allied to billowing fullness in the mouth; that is the ideal.

Among the many potential barriers to that ideal Pinot Noir in California is an overabundance of sunshine, which may ripen the grapes too quickly for them to develop subtle flavor. That has led to plantings in cool areas, like the Carneros region at the north end of San Francisco Bay and the rainy Anderson Valley of Mendocino County. Then there is the famous Chalone Vineyard, high up in the Gavilan Mountains of Monterey County. This winery's Pinot Noir, like its Chardonnay, sets a lofty standard.

All the above microclimates can produce Pinot Noirs that at their best get very close to the real thing. But the promised land for American Pinot Noir appears to be beyond the borders of California. Oregon is in the forefront, with a spate of wineries making quite lovely, stylish Pinot Noirs in the Yamhill and Willamette valleys. One of these wines, from Eyrie Vineyards, vanquished an array of august Burgundian bottles in a blind tasting held in Paris in 1979. (Only a Chambolle-Musigny from the firm of Drouhin topped it.) Surprisingly, some promising examples of Pinot Noir have begun to come out of East

Coast wineries—including the tiny, isolated Sakonnet winery, near the Rhode Island coast.

Uses

A rich, rounded Pinot Noir seems to go best with foods of a like kind. A prime rib or fine aged steak is suitably opulent. Even a chuck roast or other less expensive cut of beef will take on luxury airs when served with a fine Pinot Noir. Duck and goose also seem to need the richness of this varietal. Mushrooms bear a special affinity for this wine, and the woodsier their taste, the better. Cream sauces fall into the same category. When mushrooms and cream are combined, bring out your most sumptuous bottle of Pinot Noir and you will have reached an apex of food and wine combinations.

Of those bottles labeled simply "Burgundy," you should be wary. Chances are that the Pinot Noir grape will be absent from what is sure to be a blend of several grapes. Like the prototypical Gallo Hearty Burgundy, these are never delicate wines. They are most at home over a spaghetti dinner or by the grill.

PETITE-SYRAH
Character

Brawny is the word for Petite-Syrah. The wine's inky, blue-black color is a harbinger of its strength. It looks as if it could stain the teeth, and sometimes it will. The flavor of Petite-Syrah comes at you foursquare, with no soft edges. This is the wine that defines "full body." The taste may be of tar, resin, or the barnyard.

In the best examples, it will also be touched by the spiciness of black pepper. Petite-Syrah is an impressive wine. But that impression is, more often than not, strongest at first meeting. This is because all but the most distinguished examples of Petite-Syrah suffer the flaw of one-dimensionality. There are times, however, when that character will be exactly the one you want to stand up to strongly flavored food.

The French Framework

Among the many grapes grown in the environs of the Rhône River in south central France (up to thirteen varieties are blended into Châteaneuf-du-Pape!), the true Syrah is most esteemed. But it reaches full grandeur in only two vineyards of ancient fame. One is Côte Rôtie, where it produces the most delicate wine of the Rhône. The other is Hermitage, where it produces the most massive wine of the region. These two vineyards are only a few miles apart at the north end of the region. Their soils are similar. Only the vineyard exposure differs. At Côte Rôtie, the vines get full sun only in the morning. At Hermitage, sun shines down directly all day long. That the wines can turn out so differently is an object lesson in the power of microclimates to work their very different effects on the grape. It's been suggested that Syrah (or Sirah) derives its name from the Sicilian city of Syracuse, from which it may have been brought by the Romans in the first century.

In America

Very little true Syrah is planted in America. Our Petite-Syrah, of which there is a good deal in California, is apparently a poorer cousin also known as the Duriff. By whatever name, it does share with the French grape (with the exception of Côte Rôtie) both power and a certain stolidity that is the opposite of intriguing. In the very best examples, however, the muscle is joined to a certain sleekness that is more attractive than muscle alone. Concannon Vineyard's Chilean-born winemaker, Sergio Traverso, turns out just such a wine. The old, muscular style is represented by Ridge Vineyards' York Creek bottling. And for sheer power of the fruit, nothing comes close to the small quantities (labeled Duriff) made by the remote Santa Cruz Mountain Vineyards. Of the tiny amount of true Syrah made in California, two wineries to make it regularly available are Joseph Phelps and McDowell Valley vineyards. The latter produces an intense wine from a patch of ancient wines in Mendocino County.

It is worth noting, finally, that American Petite-Syrah is not one of those wines that gain complexity and nuance with age. As years go by, it will lose the leading edge of that enormous vigor, but it won't be replaced by anything else. Petite-Syrah shares that limitation with Beaujolais, which begins with a delicious freshness and then only wilts.

Uses

Think of Petite-Syrah as the big gun you bring in as a counterforce to certain aggressively flavored foods. Charcoal-grilled steaks, branded by the grate, will overpower or neutralize your finest Cabernet Sauvignon and Pinot Noirs. But Petite-Syrah will not be vanquished. It delivers that splendid blast of flavor that will be an equal partner to your most charred steaks and chops. This affinity was borne out, a few years ago, in an experiment done by *Food & Wine* magazine at Sparks Steak House in Manhattan. A variety of fine French and American wines were sampled with the house steak. Some had exalted reputations. To the surprise of those at the table, an unsung Petite-Syrah was the wine of choice. You can also call for the wine to accompany intensely flavored beef stews and game. If you feel like a red wine with garlicky or hot Italian sausage, Petite-Syrah will handle it.

ZINFANDEL
Character

No other American wine is so endowed with Zinfandel's range of assertive, even onrushing, flavors of berry and spice. Raspberry and blackberry are the most commonly evoked of the berries. As for the spice, it is usually pepper. In the best examples of young Zinfandel, the berry qualities flood your mouth, then give way to that hint of pepper in the aftertaste.

Zinfandel can shift styles more adroitly than any other red wine. Vinified like a sprightly Beaujolais Nouveau meant to be drunk within months of the vintage, it produces a wine that could be mistaken for fresh strawberry punch. This style is a specialty of

Amador County's Monteviña Winery, which calls it "Zinfandel Nuevo." A slightly fuller, but still very fresh, version made by Phelps corresponds to a regular Beaujolais. Then comes a whole range of "zins" made in the claret style of fine Cabernet Sauvignon. Those from Ridge Vineyards, America's premier maker of "zin," are usually blended with a bit of Petit Syrah for extra body. These wines usually begin with more flavor and less finesse than the "claret" they emulate. With age, however, that snappy fruitiness mellows. The wine gathers itself together more tightly and more abstractly. You could easily mistake a mature Zinfandel for "Cab." But since it rarely achieves the total elegance of that wine, my feeling is that you shouldn't wait until it reaches that point. Drink Zinfandel young, when it is inimitable in its thrust of flavor. In most cases, four or five years from the vintage should be just right.

The single peril of Zinfandel is its tendency to be too alcoholic. This is the result of sugar content which shoots up to high levels as the grape reaches its final ripeness—sugar that will be converted to proportionately high alcohol. The problem is compounded by the fact that when harvest-time heat waves hit California, pickers scramble to get more favored grapes off the vine—Chardonnay and Cabernet Sauvignon in particular. When they finally get around to picking Zinfandel, sugar levels may have gone stratospheric. It isn't uncommon to find Zinfandels at 15 percent alcohol. No matter how full the balancing fruit flavors, that level of alcohol tends to be tiring. It can heat up the insides of your mouth, too. These wines are known as "monster Zins." And so we are led to the third type of Zinfandel—the so-called "late-harvest" style. Often sold in half bottles, these are meant for sipping after dinner, like port.

The newest fashion to which Zinfandel has lent itself is the "blush wine" craze—white wines made from red grapes. Even though the juice of the pressed grape is immediately separated from the skins, which give wine its color, a coral tint (the "blush") still finds its way into the bottle. Sutter Home Winery, of Napa, long a specialist in red Zinfandel, showed the way with the white version in the mid-1960s. By 1982, proprietor Bob Trinchero was selling all that he could make—even after building the Napa Valley's largest single stainless-steel tank to hold the wine. Dozens of other wineries now make "blush" wines. Cabernet Sauvignon and Pinot Noir are used as well as Zinfandel. The limitation of all of them is that they tend to be stripped of flavor—a result of the juice's having been separated so quickly from the skins, which impart flavor. Zinfandel manages to retain more of its character from this process than any other red grape.

The French Framework

Of all the *vinifera* grapes, Zinfandel is the only one to which the French can't lay claim. It appears to have come here via Italy. And yet it is not unappreciated by genuinely knowledgeable Frenchmen. I once took a wrapped bottle of Ridge Zinfandel to a lunch with Christian Pol Roger, co-head of a distinguished Champagne house. The spot was the Royale Champagne, an inn located on a hilltop amid the vineyards near Epernay. Only Champagne was served until, toward the end of this leisurely and splendid meal, the cheese course came—and, with it, the "mystery" wine, still securely wrapped in brown paper. Pol Roger was told only that the wine was American. He held the glass up to the sunlight pouring through a large window and fastened his blue eyes on it for a moment. Then he sipped.

"With its spiciness, its depth of flavor and its full body, this could only be a Zinfandel," he said.

"How did you know?" I asked, truly astonished at this feat of discrimination.

"No other wine tastes quite like it," he answered.

In this context, it is instructive to note the hard choice made, some years ago, by wine writer Victor Hazan. He had sold off his cellar of rare and superb wines in New York in order to start a new one in Venice, where, with his wife, cookbook author Marcella Hazan, he had bought a home. Hazan held back only two cases for shipment to Venice. One contained Chateau d'Yquem, the legendary Sauternes. The other was a case of California Zinfandel. The Chateau d'Yquem was not a surprising choice. But why the Zinfandel (which cost a tenth of the price of the great Yquem)?

"Because in Italy I can find every type of wine I could want," explained Hazan, "except for a French Sauternes and an American Zinfandel."

In America

If you spot old gnarly hillside vines as you pass through California wine country, chances are that it's Zinfandel. Throughout much of this century, it had been the grape of choice planted by farmers—especially Italian farmers. It was the choice of knowledgeable consumers as well. A catalog from Macy's wine shop in Manhattan, circa 1935, lists its own stock of Zinfandel at a price higher than that of Cabernet Sauvignon. But that situation has since reversed. As consumers chase after the chic French varietals, humble Zinfandel has been shunted aside.

The fault has lain more with the wineries than the wine. They have too often let alcohol levels get out of hand, then bottled the wine with little or no warning on the label of the "monster" within. Unsuspecting consumers pick a bottle off the shelf, expecting it to be a fully tame table wine. Instead, they get blasted back by the impact of alcohol and perhaps residual sweetness as well. That's the last time they will venture to buy Zinfandel. And so they close themselves off from a wine capable of a wider parameter of styles than any other American wine—including some that would surely please them. When Christian Pol Roger was told, at the end of that lunch in Epernay, that Zinfandel was out of favor back home, he took another sip of the one he had just praised so highly. Then he shrugged and, taking the long view, he said, "Here in France, we have a saying about such fashions: Follow the tide, not the wave."

Uses

Zinfandel has as many uses as it has styles. The light, jubilantly fruity Beaujolais style is ideal for such casual foods as picnic ham and fried chicken. It can also be a freshing apéritif wine—with the caveat that it perhaps too slurpable. You will have drunk more than you planned to by the time the dinner bell sounds. The above recommendations also apply doubly to white Zinfandels. The finer claret-style Zinfandels, which have received oak aging to give them extra body, tannin, and finesse, can be used with lamb, duck, goose, and any other richly flavored food. Pork, for some reason, resists seduction by most red wines. But Zinfandel comes closest to succeeding.

Try to avoid pairing Zinfandel with simple preparations of veal or chicken. The wine's spiciness will come on too strong with their delicate flavor. When coq au vin is made with an intense Zinfandel sauce, on the other hand, the same wine ought to be in your glass. It is also the wine that answers best the tricky question of what to drink with certain dishes with rather exotic fruit sauces that are favorites of the new American kitchen. (Examples: grilled duck with date and port sauce or smoked wild boar with currant sauce, as found in Ellen Brown's *Cooking with the New American Chefs*.)

The late-harvest Zinfandels, which can be so ungainly when they mistakenly appear with the main course, come into their own as wines to match strong cheeses. A very ripe Brie, a sharp cheddar, or a blue cheese will cancel out the nuances of a more subtle wine. But a brawny Zinfandel, like Ridge's "Zinfandel Essence," will be in its element. Like port or sherry, these same wines are especially warming after you've returned from a long walk on a brisk autumn afternoon. A bowl of nuts or dried figs ought to be within reach.

Other Grapes

Among the minor red wine grapes, Gamay (also called Napa Gamay) is perhaps best known. It seems to be the same grape that gives us French Beaujolais —though the California version is rarely as ebulliently fruity as the original. Wines labeled Gamay Beaujolais, confusingly, are apparently not Gamay at all but a weak cousin to Pinot Noir. I don't believe you'll discern much taste difference between Gamay (or Napa Gamay) and Gamay Beaujolais. None of them, in any case, seems to have the pizazz that so captivates lovers of real Beaujolais.

The Italian Barbera grape makes an honorable showing in California. It can be quite a deep, rugged wine in the hands of the few wineries that give it special care. With Italian tomato-based dishes, it is in its element. Then there is Granache, a red varietal that is best as a rosé. As in the Rhône Valley of France, it produces a raspberry-tinted wine of almost candylike fruitiness. It is the picnic wine *par excellence*.

THE WHITE WINE GRAPES

CHARDONNAY
Character

Chardonnay is to the white grapes what Cabernet Sauvignon is to the red—the most austere and yet the richest in flavor and nuance. It is one of the very few white wines that demands at least a few years of bottle age to bring out its best. When its time finally comes, you'll get that same feeling, as with the finest

Cabernet, of not one flavor but layers of flavor. Some will reveal themselves; others will remain in shadow. But you'll sense they're there. What flavors? It's for other wines to be obvious (the raspberry of young Zinfandel, the melon of fresh Chenin Blanc). Chardonnay offers us abstractions. Okay, abstractions of what, then? It depends on which Chardonnay. In the not overly ripe style, the wine will have lemony undertones, with a touch of nuttiness as it ages. Hazelnuts, perhaps.

At the other extreme are the very ripe "Chards" from California. Here, you'll get a bigger flavor impact. Tart apple is commonly evoked by the crisper versions. Those that are softer and more unctuous, can give the impression of being buttery. The very ripest examples veer to butterscotch. That component can be quite engaging, at first. But the novelty wears off quickly. Much of the best Chardonnay is aged, or in some cases fermented, in oak barrels of various sizes. This process imparts extra depth and body to the wine. If the oak is new, you'll actually pick up the scent of a saw mill in the young wine. (Some describe this scent as vanillin.) It's hard, no matter how carefully words are chosen, to do justice to a wine as abstract as Chardonnay. The final word is that it resembles only itself.

The French Framework

If you doubt the dramatic changes that sun and soil can work upon a single grape, then observe what happens to chardonnay along its three-hundred mile north–south growing axis in central France. At the

northernmost point—around Epernay, east of Paris
—the grape produces a thin, stingily flavored wine.
Most of it becomes the backbone of Champagne,
which is normally fleshed out with other wines and
with sugar. But a bit is also bottled on its own as the
still wine called Coteaux Champennois. This is wine
that only a Frenchman could love—dry to the point
of being medicinal and quite charmless.

It is not until 250 miles southward, in Chablis, that
the Chardonnay grape first comes into its own. Here
it produces a steely, or rather a stony, wine, with a
redeeming fullness. I say stony because in that fullness are hints of granite and flint. (Oddly, the best
soil of Chablis is not stony at all, but composed of
crushed sea shells. Chablis, it seems, was once under
water.)

Fifty miles further south, Chardonnay vines appear again, on the Côte de Beaune. The grapes use
the extra bit of sun they get here, on easterly-facing
slopes, to achieve an astonishing step up to ripe grandeur. At Corton-Charlemagne and in the commune of
Puligny-Montrachet, the wine combines austerity
with richness in a way it never quite manages any-
where else. The southernmost outpost of Chardonnay, some thirty miles further on, is the region of
Macon, Pouilly-Fuissé, and Saint-Véran. These wines
are certainly flavorsome. But their style tends to be
straightforward, even rustic—not to be confused with
that of the refined Côte de Beaune whites.

In America

It's often said that Chardonnay succeeds better
than any other French grape in America. That's the

sort of generalization just waiting to be ambushed by particular bottles of every other American wine of French origin. What is irrefutable is that Chardonnay in America succeeds beautifully—some would say too much so. For years, the "blockbuster" Chardonnay reigned in California. Vintners proudly vied to see who could pack the most flavor wallop into their wine. With big flavor came big alcohol. The wines excelled in competition. But at the dinner table these muscle-bound wines could wear you out. Instead of complementing a roast chicken, they stomped it.

And so the blockbuster of the seventies gave way to the "food wine" of the eighties. The same growers who had built up their Chardonnays have now stripped them down. Gone is the big alcohol and big extract. Unfortunately, flavor and personality are sometimes gone, too. In their place, all too often, is a tart, constrained wine, from which acid but no fruit peeks out—all in the name of being a "food wine."

The above is a worst-case scenario only. And it is a problem of a grape that can do too much, rather than too little. More growers get it right than wrong. In the Napa Valley, Chardonnay seems to be at its best when it is full, intense and oaky, like those of Chateau Montelena, Beringer, and Raymond Vineyards. Certain microclimates produce lighter-bodied, high-acid Chardonnays that can have the snap of a tart apple. A cluster of small wineries in Sonoma's Russian River Valley (DeLoach, Iron Horse, Mark West) and in the Mendocino's Anderson Valley (Edmeades, Navarro) make this type of Chardonnay.

At the other extreme is the great American Chardonnay that comes from lonely Chalone Vineyards, located in the Gavilan Mountains of Monterey County, two hours south of San Francisco. The 1978 Chalone Chardonnay was a wine of unparalleled beauty and intensity of flavor. Though it was the ultimate "blockbuster," it was also too majestic a wine to fault. In keeping with the new style, the throttle has been held back on recent Chalone Chardonnays.

California is no longer the sole province of fine Chardonnay. Such Washington State wineries as Columbia (formerly Associated Vintners) and Chateau Sainte Michelle have become specialists in Chardonnay (as well as other whites) in the more nimble style. The same goes for Idaho's Sainte Chappelle Vineyards. A whole range of Chardonnays now come out of the East—notably New York State's Finger Lake region and now the tip of Long Island. Anyone who doubts that exalted Chardonnay can be made on the East Coast need only have tried the 1979 Glenora. While lacking California muscle, it had a creamy intensity that put it in the class of the finest French burgundies.

Uses

The imperial presence of a full-flavored American Chardonnay finds its perfect partner in a butter-touched lobster or grill-seared salmon. Be wary that your Chardonnay does not overwhelm fishes of more delicate flavor, like flounder, red snapper, cod, and rockfish, or fresh-water trout. Better to chill a bottle of Riesling for them. A cream or *beurre blanc* sauce will give richness to the above dishes so that a lighter-weight Chardonnay will suit. Chardonnay is an ideal partner for any chicken or turkey dish—the richer the better. The same goes for veal if a white wine is preferred.

A warning: It is only too easy to fall into the habit of drinking Chardonnay to the exclusion of other white wines. Granted, no other white wine offers so much to the senses and intellect. But don't do it. Save your acts of fidelity for other spheres. Force yourself to buy Sauvignon Blanc, Chenin Blanc, Gewürztraminer, and even jug wines. You'll come back to Chardonnay with a refreshed and newly grateful palate.

SAUVIGNON BLANC (OR FUMÉ BLANC)
Character

Crisp and lean, the Sauvignon Blanc makes up in liveliness what it lacks in depth. It often sends out a scent that is uncannily like that of freshly mown, slightly wet grass. Unlike Chardonnay, this is not a wine to ponder. Its pleasure is its firmness, its sprightliness, and its straightforward fresh character. And while there's no reason to age the wine, it will hold its edge for a surprisingly long time.

The French Framework

In the Loire Valley, a number of racy, very dry white wines are made from Sauvignon Blanc. The most famous is Pouilly-Fumé—a wine through which wisps of smoke seem to curl. Or perhaps that is only power of suggestion. The dry white wines of Graves, unlike those of the Loire, are often blended with Sémillon, a grape whose smell may remind you of lanolin. That's not necessarily a compliment to any wine. But as the minority partner in a blended white Graves, Sémillon adds a touch of richness and texture that Sauvignon Blanc lacks on its own. Unlike other Sauvignon Blanc, those from the best properties of Graves ought not to be drunk young. Ten years can go by before they reach their peak of concentration.

Sauvignon Blanc, as well as Sémillon, takes on a startlingly different character in Sauternes. Allowed to remain on the vine until they contract the "noble rot" called *Botrytis cinerea*, the grapes lose their water content until nothing remains but a sweet nectar. This is the basis of Sauternes and Barsac. (Small amounts of the Muscadelle grape may be added to the blend.) It is the high acidity of the Sauvignon Blanc that helps to keep these wines from being merely syrupy. They will last for twenty years or more.

In America

As indicated above, Chardonnay is commonly considered the most successful white wine grape in America. But that honor may actually go to Sauvignon Blanc. Its achievement, of course, is more modest. As in France, the wine is crisp and pleasing, yet without the complexity inherent in Chardonnay. Sauvignon Blanc caught on in this country when, in the mid-1970s, Robert Mondavi marketed it as "Fumé Blanc." (Who can deny that it's a more evocative name than Sauvignon Blanc?) It's natural to assume that wines labeled Fumé Blanc will bear a resemblance to the extra-crisp Puilly Fumé of the Loire—a wine made from pure Sauvignon Blanc. But it isn't necessarily so, even when the bottle is in the sloped-shouldered style of the Loire. That American Fumé Blanc may well be enriched with a bit of Sémillon in the manner of Graves. And, to make matters more confusing, if you pick up a high-shouldered, Graves-style bottle labeled simply Sauvignon Blanc, it may be purely of that grape, in the spare style of the Loire. The label should tell you which it is.

Good examples of Sauvignon Blanc/Fumé Blanc are made up and down the Pacific coast. Most examples cost less than Chardonnay, as they should—though a few, like Mondavi's "Reserve" Fumé Blanc do get over ten dollars. These had better be wines of laserlike intensity. It's curious, incidentally, that despite the success of dry Sauvignon Blanc in America, Sauternes-style versions are rarely made.

Uses

Think of Sauvignon Blanc, with its thrust and vivacity, as a wine of counterpoint. It is at its classic best as a foil to raw oysters and clams. A more unlikely but quite marvelous contrast is drawn when the wine is set against goat cheese. Most red wine is in danger of picking up the cheese's gamey taste (just as it picks up seafood's fishiness). Sauvignon Blanc cleanly pierces through that rich gaminess. This is the wine for batter-fried clams or fish fillets—or fried chicken, for that matter. Its liveliness and lack of nuance also make it ideal for the apéritif called kir— white wine with a splash of crème de cassis.

JOHANNISBERG RIESLING
(OR WHITE RIESLING)

Note: It shouldn't be necessary to append either "Johannisberg" or "white" to the Riesling name on the labels. It is said that the qualification is necessary to identify the true Riesling rather than some lesser variety (i.e. Traminer, Gray or Emerald Riesling). But nobody suggests a label that says "Bordeaux Cabernet Sauvignon" or, sillier yet, "red Cabernet Sauvignon." The name Riesling ought to suffice. But custom is strong.

Character

Of the great varietals, Riesling is the lightest on its feet, so to speak. It can achieve great intensity of fruity flavor and yet not overwhelm a plainly broiled fish or the white meat of chicken. With its direct fruitiness and high acidity, coupled with its low alcohol content, Riesling is the essential summer sipping wine. It can suggest the aroma of spring flowers and the taste of summer fruit. That taste, depending on the relative dryness of the wine, can range from crisp apple to meltingly sweet apricot or peach. Sometimes you might sense in the background a touch of lime or honey. The very sweetest versions, vinified from late-picked grapes, are like nectar. Though Riesling would seem to be a wine that would fade rather quickly, it has quite a bit of staying power. It is the only great varietal that can be utterly charming and yet memorable for the delicate strength of its personality.

The French and German Framework

Alone among the great varietals, Riesling claims Germany as its original home. On the slaty slopes of the Rhine, the Moselle, and their tributaries, the grape achieves—sometimes—a magic that is unique. This magic comes out of a precarious balance between the lively fruit of the grape and its equally lively acid. It jumps to your nose and palate like the essence of spring flowers. On the Rhine, the wine is slightly fuller and more voluptuous. Think of Renoir. On the Moselle and its tributaries, it is more angular and scintillating. Think of Matisse.

The beauty of a German Riesling is dearly bought. This is the most northerly outpost of fine wine grapes. In only a minority of summers does the sun shine down warmly enough to bring the grapes to a full ripeness that rescues the wine from unpleasant thinness. When summer stretches into a long, warm fall, the best wines will be lusciously sweet as well as fruity—and yet won't loose that all-important acid backbone. Without it, they would merely be syrupy. As in Sauternes, the *Boytris* mold shrivels the grape here in the late northerly autumn. The resulting wine, with its amber tint and viscous body, can be startling, even dizzying, in its concentrated force of flavor.

Across the German border to the south, the Alsatian France, the same Riesling grape produces a wine in which sweet delicacy has been forfeited to tensile power. And while German wines traditionally retain grape sugar, Alsatian wines are normally vinified to total dryness. This makes them much more versatile at the table than the sweeter versions, though an Alsace Riesling (or sylvaner or gewürztraminer) remains eminently sippable on its own. Of late, the Germans have also begun vinifying very dry (*trocken*) Rieslings in order to gain a greater presence at the table. I'm afraid to say, based on my sampling experience with these wines, that they've taken away what had been delectable in them and replaced it with nothing very pleasurable.

In America

Riesling, more than any other varietal, is a wine that in the last twenty years has been changed dramatically by new vinification technology. I only dimly remember the California Rieslings of old. It's not a case of failing memory but of a style of wine that offers no clear-cut character that memory can latch on to. Those Rieslings were rather full but fruitless, and above all dull—the result of long aging in big wood casks. It wasn't bad wine, but it was something perhaps more unpardonable: It was nondescript.

Today's Rieslings are fermented cold. That is, the tanks in which the process occurs are refrigerated to a temperature of 45 to 55 degrees, even though the heat of fermentation would normally bring the temperature much higher. Cold fermentation means slow fermentation—as long as thirty days. The result is a wine in which the delicate fruitiness is preserved to the maximum. The wines rarely achieve the lightness of the German paradigm. But they do have that same precise, even precarious, apposition of pointed fruitiness and zingy acid.

Fine Rieslings are made in both the West and East. The most authentic touch seems to come from wines made in Washington and New York. A Riesling of dramatically intense flavor is grown in the stony and cool Arroyo Seco microclimate of Monterey County. And some spectacular late-harvest versions are made nearly every year in California. Freemark Abbey's Edelwein was the first to earn its spurs in this category. Chateau Saint Jean in Sonoma and Joseph Phelps in Napa have been the wineries that have recently achieved the most with these wines, meant for savoring sip by tiny sip. American winemakers, thankfully, resist unwieldy German label language. So, instead of the very sweet beerenauslese, look for "Selected Late Harvest," and for the sweetest riesling of all, look for "Individual Bunch Selected." These wines—nectars, really—are made from grapes containing up to 40 percent sugar and at bottling still retain 20 percent of that sugar.

Uses

I believe that American Riesling, like the German original, is best when it retains a bit of the sweetness, which most of us begin to sense, the technicians tell us, at a natural sugar level of about .75 percent. At double that level, the wine can express its full surge of fruitiness and yet not be cloying with food. Which food? Scallops or crab meat, with their delicacy and seeming sweetness, are the match of inspiration. Fish of comparable character—tilefish, monkfish, and freshwater trout, for example—also "take" to Riesling rather than a more severe or heavier wine. The same goes for a simple dish of pasta sauce with slowly simmered sweet onions (recipe in Marcella Hazan's *More Classic Italian Cooking*).

It's no problem to admire a dessert Riesling. The problem is knowing when. To let these wines show their exquisite best, keep them away from desserts containing added sugar. That means cookies, cakes, even fruit tarts. But the wine picks up a subtle counterpoint from fruits that are low in acidity—raspberries, ripe peaches, and apricots, in particular.

GEWÜRZTRAMINER
Character

This is the grape with character in spades. In any blind tasting, it would be the wine most easily identified. It's the spice (*gewürz* in German) that does it. Roses, pepper, and cloves seemed to be mixed in its scent and taste. It can make you think of a Riesling that's been doctored up. But "gewürz" is very much itself.

The French Framework

Gewürztraminer reaches a state of powerful perfection in Alsace. At first taste, its abundance of spicy flavor makes you think the wine might be slightly sweet. But then comes a pleasingly bitter aftertaste. In a ripe year, however, the Alsatians do make genuinely sweet Gewürztraminers, which they label *vandage tardive* ("late harvest"). These wines, even more than the dry versions, need at least several years to come into their own. A decade after being late-picked, for example, the 1976 Alsatian Gewürztraminers are only just now mellowing enough to be enjoyed. It's been worth the wait.

In America

The steely, bone-dry intensity of the Alsatian model has somehow eluded American winemakers. Our Gewürztraminers seem to be most comfortably themselves when they are flowery and off-dry (e.g. Clos du Bois and Pedroncelli). Even then, the wine often retains the hint of bitterness in the aftertaste. As with Riesling, Gewürztraminer has produced superbly intense dessert wines in California. Some of the best have come out of tiny Navarro Winery in the cool Anderson Valley. Fine Gewürztraminer also is coming out of the Pacific Northwest.

Uses

Gewürztraminer is to be used warily, given its propensity to push aside whatever is in its path. It is safest as a sipping wine—especially with hors d'oeuvres that have a touch of spice themselves. After that, it's a problem. The Alsatians match "Gewürz" to their meat and cabbage dish called chou-croute garni. It's a good wine to match with pork. Gewürztraminer can also come into play in the tricky effort to match a wine to a poultry or meat stuffing that includes apples, raisins, and other dried fruits. Any dish that is animated by the forceful taste of fresh ginger is also a likely candidate to be partnered by Gewürztraminer. That includes Chinese food.

OTHER GRAPES

As wineries joust to displace one another for the customers' attention, grapes become like soldiers. The strong ones survive to stand proudly on retail shelves, while the weak are shunted to the rear or disappear altogether. Most of these vanquished grapes deserve their fate, but a few others deserve better.

Among the lesser white wine grapes, one of my favorites is French Colombard, a grape that usually is submerged into jug wine blends. On its own, it can be a strikingly perfumed and lively dry wine. The august Chalone Vineyards once made a marvelous French Colombard under the Gavilan label, but no more. Sémillon is an assertive wine that is most often used to give an extra dollop of richness to Sauvignon Blanc. You'll know why if you taste it on its own. Sémillon has a smell and taste that summons up both figs and lanolin—not tamed, as in hand cream, but pungent as in raw wool. The Muscat Canelli is another assertive grape. But it is all sweet floweriness. As a summer sipping with a bowl of ripe fruit close by, it is ideal.

The chenin blanc grape gives a wine in California which is as beguiling as that from its home vineyards along the banks and branches of the Loire River in central France. When fully ripe and slightly sweet, chenin blanc suggests ripe honeydew melon. "Serious" versions that have been vinified totally dry lose that lovely character, while gaining no offsetting assets that I've ever perceived. Another ripely-scented white that is best when slightly sweet is Emerald Riesling. Developed in California, it will thrive in heat which would flatten the real riesling. And while the latter grape can claim the purest bloodline, it is Emerald Riesling which makes, occasionally, the best impression. Paul Masson has long had a special way with this grape.

The origin of Seyval Blanc is different from others in this book. It is neither a *vinifera* grape imported from Europe, nor a purely American grape. It is a hybrid of the two, bringing the flavor qualities of *vinifera* to the hardiness of American root stock. It needs that hardiness to survive brutal winter cold spells in the East, where it is almost exclusively planted. Many hybrids have been developed, both red and white. But Seyval Blanc, with its pleasing leanness, has become most popular. Eastern winemakers are learning to make better wines from it every year. The version made by Maryland's Montbrey vineyard was included by John and Elin Walker, wine editors of *Food and Wine* magazine, as one of the dozen most memorable wines they drank in 1984. Lots of very great names in the wine world never made the list.

FIFTY
BASIC
QUESTIONS
AND
ANSWERS

THIS is a quick-study unit into which have been compressed information and opinions from elsewhere in the book. If you have time to read only one chapter, this is it.

WINE IN AMERICA

Q: *Why the focus on American wines?*

A: Because our wines, and our wine scene, are currently the most interesting on earth. All over the country, men and women have deserted other callings in order to make wine. In Europe the craft of winemaking is passed down from one generation to the next. Here, new blood is at work everywhere. Instead of trying to write the great American novel, it's become the fashion for intrepid souls to try to create the great American wine. Their struggle becomes our pleasure.

Q: *Do the best domestic wines come from California?*

A: Ninety percent of American wines come from

that state, including most of the best. But California does not have a lock on superior wines. Superb examples come from the Pacific Northwest, and from states as diverse as Idaho, New York, Pennsylvania, Maryland, and Virginia. Each year these wines get only better—though the delicate process of "fine-tuning" can't be rushed any more than can the cycle of the seasons.

Q: *Can American wines be compared with French wines?*

A: Even when vinified from identical grapes, American wines and French wines usually turn out quite differently. That's because of the unique sensitivity of the grape to differences in sun, soil, and the winemaker's hand. So don't be too intent on judging which country's wines are objectively "better." Take each on its own merits and you'll double your pleasure. But do remember that it was the French who, over hundreds of hardworking years, have set the standard by which we judge the quality and pleasures of wine. They didn't push that standard on us. We chose it. So give credit where it is due.

WINEMAKING, WINE TYPES

Q: *What are the essentials of winemaking?*

A: Grapes are normally harvested when their sugar contents reach 21 to 24 percent. They are crushed and destemmed at the winery. Then living yeasts are allowed to feed on the grape sugars in the "must," as the juice is called. Enzymes in the yeasts convert the sugar into alcohol and carbon dioxide, plus an astonishing range of hundreds of other compounds. Fermentation is a violent and primordial process. The vat of juice boils and bubbles. Put your hand close and you'll feel heat. If the yeasts are allowed to continue their work until all the sugar is gone, the wine is "dry."

If the fermentation is stopped before that point, residual sugar leaves the wine off-dry. (You perceive sweetness in wine when sugar reaches about 1 percent.) White wines are usually fermented at cool temperatures to preserve the fruitiness of the grapes. Red wines are fermented at higher temperatures to extract the most flavor from their skins. The best reds, and some of the best whites, are then aged in oak barrels prior to bottling. This process imparts tannins to the wine, which gives it extra flavor, depth, and a certain bitterness, which time will mellow.

Q: *What is the actual difference between red and white wine?*

A: The juice of both white and all major red wine grapes is colorless, or nearly so. It is the pigment in the deep purple grape skins that gives red wine its dark color. Flavor also comes primarily from the skins, which are allowed to ferment with the juice. White wine grapes are normally separated from their skins before fermentation begins.

Q: *How does a rosé wine get its color?*

A: Red wine grapes make a rosé. But their skins are allowed to remain with the juice only long enough to impart that "in-between" color. So-called "blush" wines like white Zinfandel get even less skin contact than rosés, resulting in the barest coral tint.

Q: *How does a sparkling wine get its bubbles?*

A: By the trapping of carbon dioxide gas (CO_2) in the wine during fermentation. In the making of a still wine, that gas is allowed to escape. In theory, CO_2 could be injected into still wine to make bubbles, as it is injected into soft drinks. But no American sparkling wine is made this way.

Q: *What is the difference between table wine and fortified wine?*

A: They both start out as table wine. But when a dose of brandy is added—either during or after fermentation—the result is a fortified wine. Sherry, port, and madeira are the old-world models. All three have long been copied in America—often very well. Fortified wines range between 18 and 21 percent alcohol. They are sometimes called dessert wines. That isn't necessarily an accurate designation, since dry sherries are best as apéritifs. On the other hand, "fortified" is not a word that fully pleases. To some people it sounds like what "winos" drink. (e.g., Gallo's "Thunderbird") But the term is accurate. In *The Book of California Wine,* Darrell F. Corti points out that the most engaging term for such wines is the Spanish *vinos generosos* or Portuguese *vinhos generosos:* "generous wines."

Q: *One hears constantly about varietal and generic wines. What is the difference?*

A: Varietal wines are those sold by grape name—e.g., Cabernet Sauvignon, Chardonnay. Generic wines are blends to which are given descriptive names like "hearty burgundy," "chablis," or "rhine wine." Such wines usually have little or no resemblance to the famous wine regions they allude to. In an effort to be more straightforward, some years back Robert Mondavi insisted on calling his generics simply "Red Table Wine" and "White Table Wine." Generic wines are blended of grapes in any combination the winery chooses. Varietal wines, according to federal law, must contain at least 75 percent of the named grape.

Q: *Which grapes produce the best wine?*

A: Though wine can be made from any of the thousands of species of grapes, it is those of the *vinifera* ("wine-bearing") family that turn out to be most rewarding once they are fermented and in the bottle. *Vinifera* came as cuttings to America from Europe. Among its white varieties are Chardonnay, Sauvignon Blanc, Riesling, and Muscat; and Cabernet Sauvignon, Pinot Noir, Merlot, and Zinfandel among the reds.

Q: *What about native American grapes?*

A: Some are made into wine—notably those of the family *labrusca*. The most famous grapes of this family are the red Concord and the white Catawba. They make wines of striking, even forceful, smell and taste. Though impressive the first time around, they don't have what I call the "inner dance of flavors" that would hold your interest over the long term as *vini-*

fera does. You might say that *labrusca* is too often touched, or perhaps I should say cursed, by a "lolli-pop" character.

When *vinifera* and *labrusca* are hybridized, the resulting grape produces wines of real interest—especially the clean, spritely white called Seyval Blanc. These French-American hybrids were developed for Eastern vineyards, where brutal winter weather can kill the more delicate *vinifera*. The hybrids can't yet compete with the best *vinifera* wines, but they are not to be snubbed by anyone with a real curiosity about wine.

QUALITY, COST, AGE

Q: Is a wine labeled varietally always better than a generic

A: Not anymore. For years, California winemakers aiming for the best quality were proud to make single-grape varietal wines only—especially the prestigious Cabernet Sauvignon. But recently, more attention has been paid to the Bordeaux tradition of "cutting" the hardness of Cabernet Sauvignon with the softness of the Merlot grape or the Cabernet Blanc. This can give the wine a more interesting aroma, texture, and taste. But since the proportion of "Cab" may fall below 75 percent, the wine can no longer be called Cabernet Sauvignon. It has become a "generic." That goes even for a super-luxury wine like "Opus One," the Napa Valley blend carrying the signatures of both Robert Mondavi and Baron Philippe de Rothschild. This wine, retailing for about fifty dollars, is as expensive and as esteemed as any in America. Yet for labeling purposes, it is classified exactly like a cheap jug of "burgundy."

Among the fine whites, the tangy Sauvignon Blanc (also called Fumé Blanc) is often blended with richly intense Sémillon to give a more rounded wine. The major wine grapes that are not traditionally blended are Pinot Noir, Chardonnay, and Riesling.

Q: *What is the ideal alcohol level in wine?*

A: Table wine is defined for taxation purposes as having an alcohol level of 10 to 14 percent. Red wines rarely drop below 12 percent. Light white wines, such as Chenin Blanc and especially Riesling, are best when their alcohol ranges between 9.5 and 11 percent. If there is any one drawback to California as a wine-growing region, it is an abundance of sunny days, which tend to ripen grapes to high sugar levels. That sugar must then be converted to high alcohol levels in the wine. Conversely, the increasing success of wineries in the Pacific Northwest and on the East Coast is largely due to European-style weather, which gives wines that are higher in certain acids and lower in alcohol.

ON COST AND QUALITY

Q: *How can you explain the enormous differences in cost between wines?*

A: You can't—at least, not in fully objective terms. The basic chemical composition of Gallo's Cabernet

Sauvignon, priced at about four dollars, is essentially the same as that of Robert Mondavi's Cabernet Sauvignon "Reserve," priced at twenty dollars or more. Even the bottles (costing about fifteen cents) are interchangeable. But while the chemistry of wine is objective, the pleasures of wine are subjective. Slight but telling differences in smell and taste that are apparent to your nose and palate, if not to the instruments, do exist. And, as in all else, people do pay willingly for an aura of exclusivity.

Q: *Are some wines markedly more expensive to produce from others?*

A: In wines, as in cars, you choose between mass and custom production. Gallo produces a few million bottles of wine daily at its huge Modesto "factory"— the biggest on earth. The whole process is precisely automated, beginning with machine pruning of the vines and machine harvesting of the grapes and ending with the sealing of bottles, which have been manufactured in Gallo's own factory. The result is decent, if impersonal, wine at a very good price.

At the other extreme is the class of wines made from grapes that have been raised and harvested by hand. The viticulturist fusses over each vine, pruning, trellising, and training as if it were a backyard rosebush. Picking the ripe fruit may be done not only cluster by cluster but berry by berry. The most painstaking growers pay their pickers by the hour rather than by the box, so that the incentive is to pick carefully rather than in quantity. This makes the grapes far more expensive than those that have felt only the blade of a machine. (Mechanical harvesters sometimes "pick" stones, mice, and other unlucky small animals as well as grapes.)

A custom winery may grow or buy only enough grapes to make a few hundred cases of a particular wine. It will have been vinified with the same undivided love as that of a parent. If all went well, that wine will have a special intensity, elegance, and personality of its own. That's what you pay for. Be assured that though the wine is expensive, the winemaker will never get rich by selling it, because he can never make enough of it. Nor does he necessarily want to. That's the nature of an artisan's work. To get back to the original comparison, there's no practical reason to buy a Rolls-Royce when the basic family station wagon will get you to the supermarket at least as well. Nor is there a practical reason to buy a fine, distinctive wine when an inexpensive and standardized bottle will also get you through the meal. But if choice of wine were a purely practical matter, it wouldn't be a subject worthy of more than your marginal interest.

Q: Are you scorning mass-produced wine?

A: Only a snob and a fool would do that. America (and Gallo in particular) has set the world standard for impeccable standards in "jug" wine. And that lonely fellow in his little winery is perfectly capable of making wine that is dreadful as well as superb. So you make your choice. You can buy a standard wine, knowing it will be competent but uninspiring. Or you can buy a wine that is stamped by the vision of a "custom" winemaker. Each has its place.

Q: *What is the difference between a sparkling wine at four dollars and one at several times that?*

A: The classical method of making sparkling wine was invented and perfected over centuries in the French Champagne region ninety miles east of Paris. It is exceptionally labor-intensive. Each bottle gets hand nursing. American sparkling wines made according to the *method champenoise* are priced accordingly. But shortcuts in the process were developed long ago—some by the French themselves. One of them, the Charmat bulk process, is used by Gallo to make about ten million cases of sparkling wine yearly. The bubbles are produced in huge, pressurized tanks rather than in the bottle itself, as in *method champenoise*. You needn't be ashamed to serve a well-made "Charmat" process sparkler like Gallo's "Andre." It does its job honorably. One of the better values in American *method champenoise* wine is Korbel's admirably made and reliable Brut. When priced under ten dollars, it is cheaper than any true champagne.

Q: *What is the place of a "fancy" versus a plain wine?*

A: The best wines need food that will let them shine and a few friends that appreciate them. There's no point in offering a wine that's been lovingly made and patiently aged to people who will gulp it down without a thought. That's a waste. And there's no point in serving that special wine with a dish that will blunt its fineness. Pasta with an acidic tomato sauce, for example, will do just that. The more intense and piquant the sauce, the more thorough will be the defeat for the wine. A lesser wine, with a blunter and perhaps sweeter flavor, will stand up much better to that dish. Use only standard wines, too, at parties and picnics, where they won't get any more attention than they deserve.

Q: What makes a wine good?

A: Good grapes are the *sine qua non* for good wine. But they can't overcome inadequate winemaking. To our taste, wine is good when all major components are in balance. In a white wine, that balance is between fruitiness and acidity. Fruit gives the wine flavor. Acids, of which there are at least forty in wine, give it liveliness. If fruit overwhelms acid, a dry wine will taste flat and a sweet wine will taste syrupy. If acid overwhelms fruit, the wine will be too tart. The same balance holds for red wines. But when red wine (and some whites) has been aged, or even fermented, in oak barrels, a new element enters that balance— astringent tannins and assertive flavor imparted by the wood. Wine aged in new barrels can have the vivid smell of oak chips freshly fallen from the blade. If the flavor of the wine is not sufficiently deep and intense, that oakiness will throw off the balance of the wine. One other element that must be balanced in both white and red wines is the degree of alcohol. Too little and the wine will lack impact. Too much and the wine will be ponderous and, after repeated sips, fatiguing. Some of us also get a burning sensation in the back of the mouth.

WINE AND FOOD

Q: Is it true that red wine must be served with meat and white wine with fish?

A: No wine rule is true across the board (except, in my experience, that pickles *always* ruin the taste of wine). But this oft-stated policy applies more often than not. Red meats are always best with red wine. Delicate, white-fleshed fish always needs white wine. But pale meat, like veal, goes beautifully with a full-flavored white wine like Chardonnay. And "dark" fish, like salmon or fresh tuna, is well partnered by a fruity but not too forceful red wine, like a gentle Gamay or Pinot Noir.

Q: Is there any dish that goes with all wines?

A: The most versatile dish by far is a simple roast chicken. Serve it with any wine you like—red, white, rosé or "blush," fancy or plain. The bird will honor them all. A suggestion: Since chicken is "polite" to shy wines, there's no point in serving muscle-bound wines like Petite-Syrah or a Zinfandel brimming with spice. Save them for dishes with more assertive flavor, like stews or grill-seared meats.

Q: Is there any wine that goes with all dishes?

A: No. And neither should there be. An "all-purpose" wine would deprive you of the pleasure of thinking out your next match of wine to food. (It's sometimes said that a sparkling wine goes with anything, anytime. That's overstating the versatility of bubbles.)

Q: *What about wine with cheese?*

A: Beware of this oft-praised combination. It takes a strong wine to stand up to a strong cheese. Aristocratic red wines will be wiped out by a sharp cheddar, muenster, blue cheese, or a Brie ripe enough to ooze on the plate. Don't force them to make the sacrifice. It takes young, forceful, and tannic wines to stand up to those cheeses. This is where a powerful California Zinfandel comes into its own. More subtle wines can be served with creamy cheeses, including Brie, as long as they are mild. Goat cheeses, because of their gaminess, are best served with a forceful, sharp-edged white wine, like Sauvignon Blanc. One cheese that is a uniquely considerate partner to even a subtle wine, whether red or white, is a well-aged Parmesan. The more crumbly at the edges, the better. (It's got to be the real thing, though. Non-Italian imitations won't do.) Remember, finally, that wine and most cheeses are the products of fermentation. According to the Chinese principle of yin and yang, they don't really go together.

Q: *What is the ideal wine to drink with Chinese food?*

A: Western wine evolved to complement Western food. The magnificent, multiple cuisines of China sing, so to speak, in a different key. Their basic flavoring agents—soy sauce, ginger, fermented black bean, hoisin sauce, peppers—are not calibrated to our wines. The spicy hot food of Szechwan and Hunan will actually destroy any and all wine flavor. Drink beer instead. Cantonese-style food, with its delicacy, will allow a fruity, rather delicious wine like Chenin Blanc, "blush" Zinfandel, or Gewürztraminer (it likes ginger). Best all-around: cheap sparkling wine. Even when you achieve a tolerable match between Western wine and Oriental food, you'll still miss the sequence of dishes and wines that form a traditional dinner.

Q: *What wine goes with soup?*

A: Wine is best when it makes a contrast with food texture and taste (e.g., a full, piercing red with a mild creamy cheese) or emboldens the flavor of a delicate dish (e.g., sweet water trout with a scintillating, fruit-surging Riesling). Two liquids do not a contrast make. The American wine authority Peter Quimme suggests an exception: Serve sparkling wine with soup, preferably cream-enriched. The contrast between active and still liquids can be pleasing.

Q: *Is there a place for sweet white wines at the dinner table?*

A: Don't assume that "dessert" wines automatically go with dessert. Too often, neither does much for the other. Chocolate desserts, for example, are particularly miserable partners to sweet wine or any other. There are other combinations however, that do work. You might serve a sweet Riesling or sauternes-style wine with a fruit tart that isn't overly sweet, with a crème brule, or with fresh fruit. Sweet potatoes and a dessert wine, believe it or not, do wonders for each other. Most smashing of all is the combination of blue cheese with a sweet wine. The unctuous sweetness of the wine is a perfect foil for the salty, pungent taste of the cheese. Telling you this, however, won't do you

any good. Buy a bottle of sweet Riesling or Gewerz-
traminct (the label will indicate residual sugar of at
least three percent), a wedge of blue cheese and
crusty bread. Then see for yourself.

The above sweet white wines tend to be low in
alcohol—usually about ten percent. A more potent
alternative is a pair of moderately fortified wines
called Essencia and Elysium. They are made by
Quady, a California dessert wine specialist. Essencia
is made from the Orange Muscat grape, Elysium
from the Black Muscat. These wines deliver a surge
of flowery perfume and flavor to match. Quady lightly
fortifies the two wines with brandy to bring them up
to 15 percent alcohol. A simple pound cake will allow
these two unusual wines to shine.

No matter how delicious the dessert and how beguiling the sweet wine, I must say that for me the
combination never really clicks. Would you choose to
wash down a chocolate mousse with a strawberry
milkshake?

*Q: How can sparkling wine be used to best advan-
tage?*

A: It is marvelous at both ends of a meal—as a
stimulant to appetite at the aperitif hour and as a
mouth freshener after dessert. Soups, hams, smoked
fish and oriental dishes are among the foods which
succeed with sparkling wine when other wines fail.
We are most grateful for a sparkler, however, when its
presence seems least likely, as on a thumb-twiddling
Saturday afternoon when bad weather has kept you
at home. That's the time to break out the "bubbly"—

provided you can share it with at least one other adult.

Q: *What are the truly important aspects of matching wine to food?*

A: Don't overwhelm delicate food (steamed flounder) with powerful wine (an oaky California Chardonnay). Don't eradicate the pleasures of a subtle wine (a Long Island Cabernet Sauvignon) with strongly flavored food (boiled beef in a pool of horseradish sauce). Remember that simply prepared foods show off fine wines best. Spicy or fruity sauces are best met by a spicy or fruity wine. Here are a few particularly fortuitous wine and food matches: a crisp Riesling, just touched by sweetness, with cracked crab; a full buttery Chardonnay with lobster; Cabernet Sauvignon with roast lamb; Pinot Noir with medallions of beef in a mushroom sauce; port-style wines with nuts and sharp cheddar. Listen to your mouth. It will inform you of other special affinities. And match wine to the weather as well as to food. A big red wine is wrong on a humid summer evening—and very right when the cold winds blow. Keep luncheon wines light.

BUYING WINE

Q: *Wine stores intimidate me. What should I know about them as a shopper?*

A: The basic cause of your intimidation—all those different bottles lining the shelves like regiments of soldiers—is what will pleasurably fascinate you as you learn more about wine. There are major differences among wine shops. Some merely sell wine. Others love the wine that they sell. How can you know which is the case? By inquiring where the wine stock is stored. A serious proprietor will maintain a true cellar or an air-conditioned warehouse to keep the stock in peak shape. He will also have on the floor somebody who is first a wine lover and then a salesperson. This person is likely to babble on about wine. Don't hesitate to break in to get your questions answered.

Q: *What is the retail markup on wine?*

A: Fifty percent is normal. But unlike dresses at Macy's, age-worthy wine is marked up rather than down as time passes.

Q: *Should I take advantage of case-lot discounts?*

A: All of us who love both wine and a bargain are tempted to buy single wines at case lot prices—what retailers call a "straight" case. But unless an unusually high volume of wine is consumed in your household, these cases will rapidly begin to "back up." And, more the point, you will be drinking twelve bottles of a single wine when you could be drinking, say, three bottles each of four different wines. That's much more interesting. So try to resist the lure of straight cases. But, by all means, take advantage of the discount on "mixed" cases.

RESTAURANT WINE

Q: *Ordering wine in a restaurant intimidates me even more than trying to master a wine shop. What are the essentials?*

A: Before all else, relax. Not infrequently, your waiter will know even less than you do about serving wine. You'll be presented with the cork from the bottle you've ordered (presuming the waiter managed to pull it) without having the least idea that this is a useless ritual left over from another era. Don't worry about ritual. Your main challenge will be to select wine for the diverse dishes that may have been ordered. It's not like at home, where everyone is served the same meal. A considerate wine list will include half bottles as well as carafes of various sizes. That way a couple can order both red and white wine without overindulging. In the rare case that a bona fide sommelier (wine steward) is on hand, make use of his expertise at matching menu to wine list.

His tip should be about 15 percent of the price of the bottle—but only if help is freely and accurately given and he has personally brought your selection.

Q: *How much do restaurants mark up wines?*

A: Restaurants *should* price most of their wines at no more than double the current wholesale cost. The least expensive wines could be a bit more—a bottle costing the restaurant three dollars, say, would be fairly priced at seven or eight dollars. The most expensive wines should have lower markups. A "boutique" Chardonnay that wholesales for twelve dollars, for example, needn't cost more than nineteen dollars (though it usually will). Glassware and service cost no more for an expensive bottle, after all, than for a cheap one. If the wine list seems very overpriced, respond by not buying wine. It's okay for a list to include wines at knockout prices—as long as it also includes wines at reasonable prices. There's no excuse for any list not to have a decent red and white wine for about ten dollars. If Park Avenue's fabulous The Four Seasons can do it, so can any other restaurant.

Q: *What if I think a restaurant wine tastes bad?*

A: If the sample of wine the waiter has poured for you seems "off," my suggestion is to have a second sample poured for another person at your table. If the two of you concur, your position will be more forceful. Tell the waiter what is objectionable. It is his obligation, or at least that of management, to serve a wine that pleases you. So there should be no question about taking it back. The stickiest question is whether to order another bottle of the same wine or switch. Unless the waiter resolutely insists that the next bottle of the same wine is sure to be good, you're better off not tempting fate once again.

YOUR VINOUS EDUCATION

Q: *What is the best way to learn about wine?*

A: Sip and then read. If you have enjoyed a fresh, spirited Chenin Blanc made by Parducci Winery in

Mendocino County, make it a point to read up on that varietal, the winery, the locale. Inquire into the wine's origins in the Loire Valley of France. Next time out, buy an Anjou, Coteaux de Layon, or other Chenin Blanc from that area. How does it compare with the Parducci? Since this wine came from a northerly California clime, seek out one now from "down south," like that of Monterey Vineyards. Read a little more. You'll be regularly counseled to drink Chenin Blanc as young as possible, while its fruitiness still surges. Then go to a best wine store you can find and perhaps you'll come across a French Anjou from 1969, 1959, or even 1949. For the price of an eating out for two, you can take that bottle home. Slice up a sweet peach to accompany sips of a wine that, while ancient, should be filled with flavor both steely and honeyed. You'll remember that interlude far longer than the dinner you didn't go out for.

Q: *In learning about wine, how useful are comparative tastings?*

A: No better method for sharpening your wine senses exists than to taste in succession two or more different wines made from the same grape. They could be wines from different vintages of a single winery (vertical tasting) or wines from different wineries of the same vintage (horizontal tasting). You'll be startled to find that differences you never before noticed will suddenly loom large. Compare, for example, a light-bodied, delicate Chardonnay from Mendocino County, the Pacific Northwest, or the Middle Atlantic coast with a heavy-bodied, voluptuous Monterey County Chardonnay. They will seem worlds apart. Comparative tastings are most informative when half a dozen people or so are on hand. But two people and as many half bottles also make an efficient tasting.

Q: *Should I take and keep notes?*

A: By all means. In searching for a few concise words on the appearance, smell, and taste of each wine you sample, you'll hone your powers of discrimination. And by keeping a wine log (a personal computer has replaced the legal-sized paper on which I once typed my own log), you'll be keeping company with nearly all professional tasters and serious amateurs. (It will be especially interesting to check your note on a wine you are sampling again after a lapse of many months or even years.

VINTAGES AND AGING

Q: *How much attention should I pay to vintage charts when buying wine?*

A: In some years, grapes in the northerly growing climes of France and Germany never ripen properly. Or harvest rains dilute the grapes. A vintage chart will warn you of such years—and you would do well to pay heed. California presents a different situation. Grapes always ripen fully even in the coolest viticultural regions of the state, so you need not look anxiously to a vintage chart to see if a particular year brought catastrophe to California wine. So far, it never has. The fact that there are no "bad" vintages had led, however, to the widely held belief that all California vintages are similar. They are not. Each growing season stamps the grapes with its own character. Cabernets from 1980, for example, tend to be ripe and heavy. "Cabs" from 1981 are on the light and charming side. But even these generalities tend to fall apart from one microclimate to the next. So there's not too much point in carrying a California vintage close to your bosom when you enter a wine shop.

Q: *Does it make sense to buy wines that need long aging?*

A: Don't be quick to accept the belief that red wine isn't of top quality unless it needs to molder in your basement for a decade or more in order to taste good. Cellaring French wines, which are so often born nasty, may be necessary to bring out their best. But American wines are different. More often than not, they are born smiling. They nearly always taste better than French wines at an early age. And some may taste even better in years to come. But others will simply remain as they were or begin to lose their vivacity of flavor. In sum: If it tastes good, drink up.

Q: *You mean I can't buy a case of American wine from my child's birth year to put away for her (his) wedding?*

A: Of course you can. But you'd be wiser to put way a case of old-fashioned, tough Bordeaux instead. Or, if the birth year is also declared a vintage year in Portugal, make it real port. If you insist on an American wine, you might do best to try one of the vintage ports made by the handful of California wineries that are specialists in these long-lived wines.

Q: *What is the ideal environment for long-term wine storage?*

A: You can't do better than a deep, dark, and quiet cellar where the temperature hovers perpetually around 55 degrees. In such an environment, wines have been known not only to last for a century or more but even to maintain youthful color and flavor. Only a failed cork can do them in.

Q: *How long can wine be stored in an apartment?*

A: It depends on which wine. Red wines will do fine for several years or more in a closet or other out-of-the-way spot where the average temperature goes no higher than 70 degrees. Though red wine may age prematurely from abrupt temperature changes, it seems to handle seasonal changes with aplomb. Red wines in my own apartment have spent ten years passing from youth to glorious maturity without ill effect. Others have gotten tired in half that time. The only white wines that should be stored are Chardonnays (which can benefit from aging) and sweet wines (which are preserved by their high sugar content). Other white wines should be bought only as needed.

SERVING WINE

Q: *Is there any one best corkscrew?*

A: The best, I've found, is called "Screwpull," with

its exceptionally thin, helix-cut wire coated with Teflon. It seems to take the most wary corks by surprise, including even those determined to crumble or to retreat deep into the bottle at the touch of any ordinary corkscrew. Avoid a true cork*screw*. It will push rather than cut through the cork.

Q: *Is there an ideal glass for wine service?*

A: In theory, a jelly glass ought to do. But the fact is that fine wine deserves fine glassware. A bulbous or tulip shape will best direct the smell of the wine to your nose. Keep the capacity between seven and twelve ounces. Try to buy glasses with the thinnest possible lip. For some reason, this makes the wine taste better. Such a glass will serve for both red or white wines, but sparkling wines deserve and need their own slender glasses. A champagne "flute" will preserve the bubbles longer than a wider-lipped glass and allow you to more easily contemplate those wondrous bubbles.

Q: *What is the purpose of decanting wine?*

A: Old wines need decanting to separate clear wine from the sediment at the bottom of the bottle. Wines of all ages *may* gain in flavor by being allowed to "breathe" after decanting. Air contact is presumed to accelerate the slow process of development in the bottle from years to hours or even minutes. Does it really work? When expert tasters are asked to identify which of two identical wines has been decanted for periods of up to several hours and which has just been uncorked, they fail as often as they succeed. My advice is to sample the wine straight out of bottle. If it delivers full flavor, decant only for the pleasure of ceremony. If it seems "bitey" or lacking in flavor, decant it. Half an hour later, take a sip. You may find that the wine has blossomed out.

A
SPECIAL
DINNER

EVERY so often, the time comes to prepare a very special dinner for friends and family. Even if you have a sure hand in the kitchen, however, you may be daunted at the problem of matching not just one bottle but an array of wines to the dishes you will present.

Yet the right wines, beginning even before your guests are called to table, will elevate that meal from being merely special to one that is memorable. Months or even years later, your guests may rave more about the wines you selected than the food you prepared. That's not an insult. The right wine at the right time has a way of insinuating itself into our long-term memory in a way that food never does.

This chapter will guide you in fine-tuning food and wine for that special dinner.

THE APERITIF HOUR

Q: *I'd like to offer my guests an interesting wine — one that will even induce them to forego hard liquor. What considerations should be weighed in choosing that opening wine?*

A: Will you be sipping the wine alone or with hors d'oeuvres? This is the first factor. Certain wines are at their best on their own. Others need food to bring out their fullest pleasures. Then there are wines that can go either way. One of my own favorites for solo sipping is Gewürztraminer. It may be dry or slightly sweet. But in either case, its intimations of roses, pepper and cloves make it the most assertive of white wines. Gewürztraminer doesn't want to "relate" to most foods, just as certain guests don't relate to their tablemates. It is best appreciated when permitted to shine on its own. That makes it an ideal aperitif wine, especially when there's nothing put out to nibble.

Q: *What's an example of an aperitif wine that isn't at its best when sipped alone?*

A: Sauvignon Blanc (also known as Fumé Blanc), a wine which has been gaining favor with Americans, is the wrong wine to be sipped on its own. It has—or ought to have—a tart, herbal-tinged bite which works best as a punctuation note to certain richer-tasting foods. It is perfect, for example, for cutting the rich flavor of fresh oysters on the half-shell. (A hot, horse-radish spiked "cocktail" sauce serves the same function—but, unlike the wine, it tends to knock out the delicate, ocean-essence flavor of the fresh mollusc.) The edge of a fresh, young, grassy Sauvignon Blanc can also serve to cut the unctuousness of a fat-flecked country pâté.

Q: *What wines work equally well alone and with hors d'oeuvres?*

A: Riesling is the best example of a white wine

which goes both ways with equal grace. Though it may be intensely fruity with nuances of fresh green apples or apricots, Riesling is neither so aggressively spicy as Gewürztraminer nor so bitingly tart as Sauvignon Blanc. It marries well with foods that aren't inherently rich or assertive—chicken or turkey, for example, or less-oily fish like trout and cod, abalone and crab.

Q: What if I am serving a more oily fish—like smoked salmon?

A: It's hard to imagine how a food as delicate, delicious and as patrician as smoked salmon can utterly destroy a fine wine. But it will. Try a sip of an otherwise fresh-tasting white wine after a bite of smoked salmon and you'll get the distinct impression that somebody back at the winery had dropped a dead fish into the fermenting vat—and not a fresh fish at that. The bubbles of a dry sparkling wine, however, do seem to drive this unwanted visitation away. A sparkler is also dandy, of course, all by itself. And so pleasing to the eye.

Q: What wine goes with caviar?

A: Once again, sparkling wine is the only solution. Keep it very dry, as the fishiness of even the freshest sturgeon or salmon eggs is not kind to any touch of sweetness in the wine. The other solution is to forgo wine in favor of iced vodka.

Q: So far, you've mentioned only white wines as aperitifs. Is there any reason not to use red wine?

A: Remember that "serious" red wines are usually

fermented "on the skins," and perhaps with pits and stems as well. This imparts tannins to the wine. Additional tannins come from barrel aging. Tannin is an acid—the same as used to tan leather. It imparts an edge to these classically vinified red wines, rendering them less than ideal for sipping alone. They are meant to be served with food. Cabernet Sauvignon, in particular, can seem rather mean on a bare stage.

Luckily for those who insist on a red wine at aperitif time, there are options far less somber than the big reds. Foremost in this category are "unserious" sippers in the Beaujolais style. These wines are jubilantly fruity and untannic by both inclination and vinification. Due to confusion over which domestic grape is the closest relative to the true Gamay grape of Beaujolais, you will find California versions of these wines labeled variously as Gamay Beaujolais, Napa Gamay, or just plain Gamay. Even closer to the fresh spirit of real Beaujolais is Zinfandel, which has been vinified in its style. Montevina's version, "Zinfandel Nuevo," is almost riotous in its onrush of strawberrylike flavor.

Q: *What wine will go best with a tray of cheese and crackers?*

A: Contrary to usual opinion, wine and cheese aren't an automatic match. Certain combinations will work together; others won't. Sharp cheeses—a mainstay of most pre-meal cheese trays—tend to demand their own space. So do goat cheeses. But beyond the individual matches or mismatches is a question: should cheese be there to nibble on at aperitif time? My answer is strongly negative. Cheeses, with their density and richness, are all wrong as perks to the appetite. They'll never let you get to the dinner table with your hunger intact. Save them for the other end of the meal. That's also where the wines that will accompany them belong.

Q: *You mentioned a number of white wines to serve as an aperitif, but not my favorite—Chardonnay.*

A: Chardonnay is a wine of paradox. Of all white wines, it has the deepest, fullest, most interesting flavor. You might even say personality. You would think, given those qualities, that it would stand best on its own. But when Chardonnay is poured before dinner, you will quickly see that the power of the wine is austere. It can be a little off-putting. That austerity is best combined with food of some richness—a chicken or veal dish where the butter or cream hasn't been spared, for example. Save Chardonnay, as you would Cabernet Sauvignon, for the dinner table.

Q: *Isn't sherry a traditional aperitif?*

A: It has been the aperitif of choice since Victorian times. Through the 1960s, more American sherry was sold than any single unfortified table wine. Though white wine is now in the ascendancy, a dry sherry continues to be a very nice aperitif indeed. My only reservation is that it is not ideal to precede a meal in which fine table wines will be served. There are two problems. One is that sherry is quite high in alcohol—18 to 20 percent—while scintillating Rieslings, for instance, are currently vinified to as little as nine percent alcohol. More alcohol always means more flavor in a wine—or, at least, more impact.

When wines of lesser alcohol follow, they tend, at first sips, to seem pale, or even washed out by comparison. And first sips *do* set the tone.

The other problem with sherry is inherent in its making: Sherry undergoes long aging in barrel which results in oxidation—the taste also known as "madeirazation." That's good in sherry (or its relative, Madeira). It's bad, though, in table wine. When you shift from sherry to, say, a young Riesling with the fish course that opens the meal, the imprint of the sherry will still be on your taste buds. It won't be hospitable to that first taste of Riesling, or any other unfortified white wine.

Even the weather ought to be a factor in determining whether you will offer your guests dry sherry or other fortified wine. The effect of the extra alcohol seems to be enhanced, and perhaps over enhanced, by a warm summer evening. Sherry, port, Madeira and the like were all popularized, if not developed, by the English to warm them in their damp and drafty environs. It's not only the high alcohol drinks, incidentally, that can go to your head quickly in warm weather. Sparkling wine will do the same. The bubbles are the culprit: They seem to get the alcohol to your bloodstream with an extra rush not provided by still wines.

Q: *The above rules are fairly specific. Are there any general rules for the service of aperitif wines?*

A: Like the nibbles served during cocktail hour, the wine should merely perk our appetites. Lively acidity coupled to engaging fruitiness, low tannins and alcohol will do just that. White wines meet these specifications better than reds. Wine served with food can be drier than wine served on its own. Salty foods like country ham take well to sparkling wine. On the whole, liveliness and a slight off-dry character will be appreciated by most guests in their aperitif wine. That is exactly the type of wine—Chenin Blanc, Gewürztraminer, Johannesberg Riesling—that American wineries are adept at making.

Finally: One glass of wine and a refill will perk the appetite and the spirit. After that, it's time to move to the table.

AT THE TABLE
WINE FOR THE FIRST COURSE

Q: I'd like to show off the best possible wines all through the meal. Any recommendations on how to best do that with the first course?

A: Fish and a superior white wine traditionally open the dinner. That tradition perfectly suits American tables and American wines. Fish, with its unrivaled leanness, is very much the dish of today; but not every white wine is a suitable match.

Q: What would be an example of a mismatch?

A: Serving an ultimately delicate flounder with an oaky, forceful Chardonnay is a mismatch. The same goes for a tuna steak, marinated in olive oil and rosemary, if served with a flowery Riesling. It's not that these combinations will taste bad. It's just that the scale is out of kilter. As with matching colors, the relative intensity of each shade counts as much as the colors themselves.

Q: *Suppose I'm determined to show off a rich Chardonnay and an inherently delicate fish?*

A: Enrich the fish to match the wine. Cream and butter sauces will always give the fish the extra weight needed to match the force of the Chardonnay. They can be further enriched with mushrooms or spiked with fresh herbs like parsley, dill, or coriander. If for caloric or other reasons you want to keep the fish preparation at its unadorned simplest, then do consider a fish of inherently richer flavor that will carry the wine on its own. Fresh salmon, with its opulent character, is the obvious choice. Striped bass is another. Despite its white, less-oily flesh, bass is a powerhouse of flavor—as is shad, a fish that should not be ignored in the spring season.

Q: *What about matching wine to a soup course?*

A: The problem here is that you are trying to match two liquids. On principle, it's not a happy combination. A well-baked, crusty and chewy dinner roll is a much better companion to soup than any wine. That said, certain soups do go better with wine than others. A creamy lobster, mussel, or fish bisque can be set off nicely by a crisp white of almost any kind—though I'd be inclined to choose a fruity, off-dry Chenin Blanc or Riesling. Most vegetable soups are not especially hospitable to wine—though a mushroom soup is a pleasing exception. The English tradition is to serve a dry sherry with soup—a double consommé seems to have been the ideal. I keep promising myself to try this combination, but it's a promise that may go unkept. Following sherry with a table wine isn't, for me, an idea with great appeal. Again, the one wine that makes the maximum contrast with soup is a sparkling wine.

Q: *What about wine with pasta as a first course?*

A: Pasta has come late to mainstream America, but it has come with a vengeance—especially on up-to-date restaurant menus. Splitting an opening order of pasta has become an accepted ritual of ordering. Starting the meal with pasta works as well at home. Particularly if the main course is a red meat—beef, lamb, duck, etc.—a first course of pasta is a way of not overdoing the carnal side of the meal. The infinite variations of pasta saucings forbid any absolute rules about the accompanying wines. But a good policy is to save your best wines for other dishes—ones that are simpler and more distinctive.

A pasta dish is often concocted of too many ingredients to rivet itself to a particular wine choice. The traditional spaghetti carbonara, for example, with its blend of bacon, Parmesan cheese, cream and eggs (with perhaps a few peas thrown in), can be eaten as well with a light-bodied red wine or a wide variety of whites. The same goes for the modish pasta primavera, with its toss of seasonal vegetables.

Q: *I insist on some specific recommendations for wine and pasta matches. Linguini with white or red clam sauce, for example.*

A: A white clam sauce, with its low-tide pungency

of reduced broth of the clams, is so distinctive that it would seem to demand a particular wine. In Venice, you'd wash down this dish—spaghetti alla vongole—with a tartly thin white wine from the northeast of the country. That's one of the few types of white wine not made in California. But what wine for linguini in white clam sauce? One is spritely and simple, like French Colombard or Sauvignon Blanc. Best of all would be an East Coast Seyval Blanc, a firm but impersonal wine that wouldn't be out of place in that Venetian trattoria.

Q: *What wine for clams, squid, or shrimp in a red sauce?*

A: Red sauces, being ruled by the acidic, domineering flavor of reduced tomatoes, offer a poor welcome to all wines, so almost any wine will do. Just make sure it's not your best. This is one case in which, since there's no preferable red or white wine, a "blush" like white Zinfandel would be in order. You might also try a true rosé made from the granache—the same grape which makes the full but easygoing Tavel of the French Rhône. A superb example of Granache, surging with strawberrylike fruit, is made by Château St. Michelle in Washington.

Q: *Spaghetti with a Bolognaise meat sauce?*

A: Once again, anything but your best red. Though this is a book about American wines, I'd be tempted here to buy an uncomplicated Italian wine—red Corvo, Valpolicella, or Chianti Classico.

Q: *What wine goes with pasta in a pesto sauce?*

A: This bright green sauce—made from basil leaves, grated hard cheese (traditionally, Parmesan and pecorino), pine nuts, oil, butter, and garlic—is ruled by the distinctive, almost flowery tang of the basil leaves. It isn't particularly hospitable to wine. The best choice might be a flowery crisp, off-dry Riesling that is crisp and flowery but not too delicate —wines from the Alexander Valley (Clos du Bois, Alexander Valley Vineyards) or from Monterey County (J. Lohr and Kendall-Jackson and any wine that says Ventana). The extra bit of power in these wines is what it takes to stand up to pesto.

Q: *You've been pretty negative so far about serving fine wines with pasta. Is there no noodle dish which will bring honor to a valued red or white wine?*

A: Here are two:

1. Pasta with a cream sauce of mushrooms— not limited to the standard store-bought variety. Mix in fresh or dried wild mushrooms like the Italian porcini or French morels. Best of all would be truffles. The earthy, wonderfully deep autumnal richness of a mushroom sauce actually demands a wine of comparable depth. A very sound, suave, and velvety Pinot Noir is the perfect match. The best, like those of Acacia and Chalone Vineyards, aren't cheap. But neither are those wild mushrooms. And they do deserve each other.

2. Pasta with a Gorgonzola cream sauce. On its own, this ultra-pungent cheese will blast back all but the most powerful red wines. Mel-

lowed by cream or just plain milk, it becomes a perfectly behaved accompaniment to fine wine. I'd again pick a Pinot Noir, or a very deep Zinfandel (Château Montelena or Ridge's York Creek or Geyserville bottlings would be pricy but perfect) or one of the more fleshy, powerful Cabernets like Trefethan's. If the Gorgonzola component of the sauce is very restrained, an elegant Cabernet will also be in order—Simi's, for example, or the Beaulieu "Rutherford." A big deep Chardonnay will also work. Chateau Montelena, again, would be a fine choice, as would the less expensive version in the same full-volume style by Raymond Vineyards. The above recommendations also hold for pasta plainly with nothing more than butter and freshly grated, real Parmesan cheese. It is a dish that will be an equal partner to the most stellar wines.

MAIN COURSES

Q: *What should be considered in choosing the main course wine?*

A: If only white wine has gone before, you have now set the stage for a first-class red wine. Obviously, the entrée you serve will determine which. But it's necessary to think ahead. Is a cheese course coming? If so, you'll have to pick your red wine for the main course with an eye toward the following wine. It could be the same wine for both courses. If not, it's important that the cheese wine be the one with the most authoritative flavor. I don't mean that the earlier wine must be of lesser quality. Only that it be the more subtle of the two.

Q: *Does the food-and-wine match stand above all others for the main course?*

A: Each plate, each wine, has its own way of shining. But the classic match, I believe, is a leg of lamb, roasted on the bone to conserve its juices, served with slow cooked white beans or puréed turnips and a green vegetable like buttered green beans. The wine which marries perfectly to this dish is Cabernet Sauvignon.

Q: *If I serve a Cabernet Sauvignon with lamb, does the age of the wine matter?*

A: Both youth and maturity have their individual virtues. The young "Cab," with its tannic edge, will best cut through the rich, slightly gamey smell and taste of the lamb. An older wine, with its tannins softened by bottle age, won't provide quite that contrast. But it will offer an extra dimension of flavor complexity that only comes with the years. Either way, you will have a noble matching of a particular dish and wine. The caveat here is that American wines, and especially California wines, have not proved so reliable as French wines in improving with age. On the other hand, they are almost always more approachable at an early age. A three-year-old Bordeaux, for example, will normally be tannic and "closed up." It will take many more years before it gives up the smell and flavor for which it is justly famed. But a three-year-old California Cabernet will usually be rich with young fruit.

Q: *What is the best wine with roast beef?*

A: Roast beef—whether a rump roast or a prime rib—has an unexpected way of making Cabernet Sauvignon seem too raw at the edges. Pinot Noir, with its earthy softness, is a far better choice. The ones closest to the Burgundian ideal are coming out of Oregon vineyards like Eyrie and Tulatin. More forceful Pinot Noirs come from California, notably in the cool and foggy Carneros region of the Napa Valley. Beaulieu, Carneros Creek Winery, and the new, ambitious Acacia Winery are among those making superior Pinot Noirs in this region.

Merlot is another grape which produces wines with the soft-edged warmth that seems best to complement roast beef. Duckhorn, a newer winery in Napa, has burst forth as the Merlot specialist of America. But quite lovely versions are made by Rutherford Hill, Clos du Bois, and Sterling Vineyards. An exceptionally affable version has long been made by Louis Martini. It is always a best buy.

Q: *Does veal go with a particular wine?*

A: The delicate color and flavor of veal—it is certainly less "meaty" in flavor than dark turkey meat and much less so than any part of a duck—is too passive to take a strong stance for or against most red wines. Your most important consideration will be to match rather than overmatch the delicate character of fine veal. And, obviously, the method of preparation is critical to that selection. A plain veal chop is a per-

fect foil for any well-aged fine wine—the more delicate the better. Either a refined Pinot Noir or buttery
Chardonnay will give pleasure. For veal piccata, with
its lemony edge, you might opt for an off-dry Riesling.

Q: *Can I serve a fine wine with pork?*

A: Pork is the meat least likely to hit it off with a
top-class red wine. But some pork-and-wine combinations are better than others. For a pork roast or chops,
a Gewürztraminer should work out well. Its spiciness
seems to ride right over whatever is recalcitrant in the
pork. A rosé of Cabernet Sauvignon or a Gamay
Beaujolais will also do. Just bear in mind that wine-
and-pork combinations are not made in heaven.
Worst of all: baked glazed ham and wine. Yield here
to beer or lemonade or a low-priced, slightly sweet
bubbly like Sutter Home Vineyard's new Zinfandel
"Sparkler." Or better yet, if the season is right, fill
those mugs with apple cider. If it's turned just a bit
hard, that's all to the good.

Q: *How about some guidelines on matching wine to
poultry dishes?*

A: The birds which come to table are more various
in flavor intensity than any other group of meats.
Breast of turkey, at one extreme, can have all the flavor of roasted cardboard (especially if it's been frozen
and then overcooked). And yet few meats are so intense as dark, chewy breast of duck or leg of goose.
Falling somewhere in between these two extremes is
chicken—the most popular and least expensive form
of poultry. This diversity of birds for the table, as well
as the methods of their preparation, provides an op-

portunity to draw on the whole magnificent range of fine American wines. It's a pleasurable prospect.

Q: *Let's start basic. Does any particular wine go best with a simple roast chicken?*

A: Who says a roast chicken is so simple? Dark meat and light meat differ in taste. In theory, you would match one wine to breast meat and another to the drumsticks—and a third to the crispy skin. Lacking the ideal, however, it must be said that both red and white wines will match beautifully to the whole of a roasted bird. In general, the whites should be fuller and the reds on the more refined side. A big, buttery Chardonnay is best among the whites. A Cabernet Sauvignon that isn't too "inky" is best among the reds. Merlot is also welcome. At my table, I don't hesitate to offer my guests a choice of red or white.

Q: *Do any chicken dishes call absolutely for red wine?*

A: Many years ago, at a country restaurant in Burgundian France, I was served a *coq au vin*—chicken in wine—in which the pieces of the bird were covered in the darkest, most lustrous sauce that I'd ever experienced. That darkness came from chicken stock and red wine which had been reduced until nothing was left except its soul and pigment (and perhaps a touch of caramelized sugar). It was as lustrous and deep as ten coats of Chinese lacquer. That was a dish where only a red wine would do—and quite a powerful one. The common procedure is to drink the same wine that you've used for the sauce. My own experience suggests, however, that simple, vinous wines work best in cooking. More mature and subtle wines ought to be reserved for your glass. In the case of that *coq au vin*, which is a wonderful cold-weather dish, I'd cook down that sauce with any good jug wine and serve the dish with any firm and generous red wine that matched my mood.

Q: *Does fried chicken call for its own wine?*

A: No pleasure of the table is so pure as that of biting into a freshly fried, crispy golden-skinned piece of chicken. Yet this is a dish which we inevitably see as the ultimate in informality—the backbone of the family picnic. Fried chicken wants an easy going wine to match that character. A rosé of Cabernet Sauvignon or Zinfandel will be just right. Be sure it is well-chilled. If you're in the mood for a real red, Gamay is ideal.

Q: *What wine for turkey?*

A: The same as for chicken—unless the turkey is stuffed. Given the neutral character of this bird, that stuffing will be the controlling factor in deciding what wine to use. One of the most considerate partners to any well-matured red or white wine, incidentally, is left-over turkey, served unheated. It will allow any and all subtleties of the wine to shine right through.

Q: *How does duck rate as a wine partner?*

A: Tops. With its dense flesh, its intensity of flavor and its unctuousness, duck wants and needs an accompanying red wine of real stature and thrust. Wines which would overpower chicken or turkey will be in their own league with roast duck. No other dish, in fact, is so unfinicky when it comes to being mated to wine. It welcomes both red and white. Cabernet Sauvignon, Zinfandel, Pinot Noir, Petite-Syrah will all be in their element among the reds. A dry Chardonnay or a slightly sweet Riesling will each find their own harmony among the whites.

Q: *I especially adore duck* à l'orange. *Does this alter the wine choice?*

A: You have a problem. An orange glaze, which is both acidic and sweet, will fight a dry wine. And if it is very sweet, it will fight and win. The same goes for that other traditional partner to duck—a cherry sauce. If you addressed this problem to a château owner in the Sauternaise area of France, he wouldn't hesitate to tell you the perfect solution: serve a Sauterne, which will handle the sweetness of the sauce very well. He'd have a point, but most of us will never affront current custom by serving a dessert wine with the main course. My own choice: a young Zinfandel in which the fruit and spice haven't yet been muted.

THE SALAD COURSE

Q: *Is it true that wine and a dressed salad won't mix?*

A: We are often instructed that the vinegar in a basic salad dressing will turn any wine that is served with it. This *may* be true—especially if the dressing is made from oil and vinegar of no particular character. But if you use superior ingredients in restrained proportions (4 to 1 instead of the traditional 3 to 1), your salad and wine will show a surprising degree of mutual tolerance. The preferred oils would be a characterful, extra virgin olive oil with a tang of the fruit or a nut oil—hazelnut or walnut. Among vinegars, none excels like the dark Italian balsamic or the Spanish sherry (Romate V.O. is the brand on our shelf). At their most sumptuous, these vinegars actually give pleasure sipped from a spoon.

Serving the salad French style, after the main course, rather than American style, at the beginning of the dinner, also seems to make peace between wine and salad. Wine writer Victor Hazan has suggested that the wine goes down smoother with the late-served salad because the mouth has been coated with oils and butter from the previous courses. At any rate, it's usually a pleasure to continue lingering over the wine with the salad course. And, of course, a fresh bread, warmed in cool weather, does wonders in buffering that acidic tang which should never be banished from the dressed greens.

THE CHEESE COURSE

Q: *I look forward to wine and cheese together. And yet you've suggested that the two don't really go together.*

A: I only meant to take this pair out of the realm of automatic bliss. Be cautious. A slightly underripe Brie or Camembert, for example, will behave well with almost any fine red wine. But that same cheese, once it has turned very ripe and runny, will knock out the finer points of the wine. You will get another sort of mismatch by confronting a gentle wine with a sharp, well-aged hard cheddar like Canadian Black Diamond. The tang of the cheese, so delectable on its own, will overwhelm the wine. If you want to test this point, take a bite of that wonderful cheddar and follow it at once with a sip of a first-class Cabernet Sauvignon. For about two seconds, you won't be able to taste the wine at all. The sharpness of the cheese seems to anaesthetize your taste buds. That's not being hospitable to the Cabernet Sauvignon.

Yet another caveat: Goat's or sheep's milk cheeses —particularly soft ones like the French Montrechet —typically have a certain gaminess to them that is off-putting to red wine. An unsophisticated newcomer to a quite ripe *chèvre* at my table described the cheese as smelling like "sweaty tennis shoes from a gym locker." She was devastatingly, if not appetizingly, accurate. This gaminess, while enticing on its own, takes the graces out of fine red wine. One solution is to take a cue from the French, who often match their *chèvre* with very dry, herbal-tinged white wines like Sancerre, made from the Sauvignon Blanc grape. American versions of that grape, like those of Sterling, Mondavi, or Beaulieu will work admirably. It's not only goat cheeses that can do in a fine red wine. A tangy, slightly stinky cow's milk cheese like Leiderkranz or ripe Muenster will also do it in. (And it is inevitably the case that cheese does in the wine, not the other way around.)

Q: *So much for the negatives. Can I hear about some great wine-and-cheese combinations?*

A: Any cow's milk cheese which isn't too ripe or too tart or tangy will soften red wine and give pleasure. The creamier the better. (The very richest, like the French triple cream *Explorateur*, offer an especially dramatic counterpoint to a young, rich and tannic Cabernet or Zinfandel.) One of the noblest partners to an older red wine is an aged Parmesan reggianno, finest of this type of Italian cheese. Lately, "vintaged" wheels of Parmesan reggianno have appeared in the U.S. Typically, they are three years old. With its discolored and crumbling edges, a chunk of this cheese looks, to the uninitiated, as if it has gone totally over the hill. But its nutty, lingering flavor reaches out warmly to wine without competing with it. Try it, as you did with the sharp cheese, with a refined Cabernet. The cheese, despite its full flavor, won't block out the wine at all. Your most velvety Pinot Noir and most complex, fully matured Cabernet await this expensive but inimitable cheese.

Perhaps the most dramatic wine-and-cheese partnering brings together a tangy, salty, blue cheese with a sweet white wine. Roquefort and a Sauterne wine are the French standard. The one is salty and pungent, the other sweet and unctuous. They are opposites made for each other. Sauterne is one of the few French wines not regularly imitated in America. But we do boast naturally sweet Rieslings and Gewürztraminers in the late harvested Germanic tradition which make that same stunning contrast with a blue cheese. With the king of the English blues, Stilton, you'd best reach for Port, with its own natural sweetness and the force of a gentle giant. American versions of the Portuguese original are getting ever better. (See the discusion of dessert wines that follows.)

THE DESSERT COURSE

Q: *Is there a guideline for serving wine with dessert?*

A: The guideline is not to do it. Sweets totally spoil the pleasures of dry red or white wines and they substantially downgrade the pleasures of finely crafted dessert wines. The sugariness of cakes and pies, puddings and ice creams, seems to bring out the acid in an otherwise graceful sweet wine, throwing it out of balance with its own sugars. Chocolate, in particular, has a disastrous effect on table wines. And the deeper, the darker, the richer the chocolate, the greater the disaster.

Q: *A guideline has to have exceptions.*

A: A nut cake or torte goes well enough with a late harvest Riesling or Gewürztraminer, with a late-harvest Zinfandel or with Port. A fruit tart, particularly if made with dried fruit like prunes or figs, will also coexist well enough with the above wines. So will a sparkling wine that's not too dry. Fresh raspberries are very good at showing off a late-harvest Riesling or Gewürztraminer. You could even include a dollop of whipped cream on the berries without causing the wine to suffer.

AFTER DINNER SIPPING

Q: *Is there a best way to finish the evening's drinking?*

A: My feeling is that now is the time, after making the dessert course a wineless interval, to offer dessert wines to your guests. With nothing more than a bowl of nuts at hand, an array of American dessert wines can come into their own. It could be one of those stunningly intense late-harvest Rieslings or Gewürztraminers, with their stunningly intense aromas and tastes of apricot, honey, and pineapple. These wines —more like nectars, really—are expensive, but a half bottle is all you'll need to treat up to half a dozen people.

If winter winds blow, it's the right time to break out a fortified wine. Port is the obvious choice. A little band of California wineries—Fricklen, Quady, Woodbury, and J.W. Morris—specialize in them. Though there's an honorable attempt to make these wines with traditional Portuguese grape varieties, Zinfandel Ports have a unique spiciness of their own. I prefer them frankly, to unfortified late-harvest Zinfandels, which get their alcoholic kick not from the addition of brandy to normal wine but from overripe grapes.

Two unique dessert wines which are worth seeking out are Quady's Elysium, a red wine from the black muscat grape, and Elysium, a white wine made from the even rarer orange muscat. These are exotically lush and intriguing wines, full of ravishing fruit scents, after which nothing vinous can follow.

Q: *You mentioned earlier that champagne is traditional at the end of a formal French meal.*

A: You might think of champagne at the end of the meal the way the Chinese think of a clear soup at the end of a long banquet: it leaves the mouth clean and refreshed. A final glass of sparkling wine also has the virtue of being lower in alcohol than the fortified wines, brandies, or liqueurs. In lieu of a late-harvest white wine, this is a splendid way to end a dinner when the evening is warm.

MAKING
SENSE
OF
WHAT
YOU'RE
TASTING

T H E "expert" who has come to dinner watches as the decanter of mystery wine is presented. He has been told only that it is a California wine. It's up to him to identify the grape, the winery and vineyard, and even the vintage.. With thousands of California wines appearing each year, it seems like an impossible task.

A small amount of wine is poured in the expert's glass. His eyes rove the lights and lamps in this sedate room. Mumbling an apology, he removes the silk shade from a wall sconce. Then, tilting his glass to the bare bulb, he fixes his eye on the wine within. For several moments, he stares like that. Then, with a slight motion of his wrist, he starts the wine swirling. It goes faster and faster until there's a mini-maelstrom in the bowl of the glass. Whirling up to the rim, it threatens to go airborne. But the expert has it under precise control. Abruptly, he plunges his nose into the glass. He sniffs loudly, explosively. And now he turns his head away from the glass to a vacant corner of the room. His brow is furrowed. For all the respectful watchers know, he could be thinking of differential equations.

The expert returns his focus to the glass for one more round of raucous sniffing. Then, at last, he does what the uninitiated observer expected him to do in the first place: he actually deigns to taste the wine. Snorts are now superseded by explosive gurgles. A child would be sent away from the table for such behavior. At a restaurant, these sounds would bring a rush of volunteers eager to perform the Heimlich maneuver. Here, in the dining room, the guests merely stand in motionless awe.

After an interminable interval of these unceasing gurgles, the expert goes over to a ficus tree in a large pot. Without even leaning, he spits the whole mouthful into it—shoots it, actually, in a long crimson stream as if he were a human squirt gun.

Only now does the expert speak. "I can't be sure, of course," he says, though a curl of a smile suggests that he is quite sure indeed. "But I'll hazard a guess about the identity of this wine." He pauses. "It is a Zinfandel made by Joseph Phelps Vineyards, which is located in the Napa Valley. But the grapes actually come from the Alexander Valley of Sonoma County. The vintage is 1976."

The host's jaw drops. He extends the hand of congratulations as guests break into applause. The bottle, bearing the Phelps label exactly as described, is now brought in from its hiding place in the kitchen. Wine is poured for all—except our expert. At this moment of his triumph, he is busy screwing the shade back on the sconce.

You may smile skeptically at what has gone on above. It's all too easy to dismiss the wine-tasting ritual as so much hollow snobbery. And if wine were like all other consumable liquids, the ritual ought to be dismissed. But wine is a law unto itself—providing it is honestly made. It has, miraculously, a character of its own. It has particularity. That doesn't mean that each and every example will be especially attractive or interesting. But it will be just slightly different even from the next wine that is neither especially attractive nor interesting. Those differences won't necessarily jump out at you. You'll never notice unless you pay close attention. And that's all our expert has done: paid close attention to what he has seen, smelled, and tasted in the glass of "mystery" wine at hand.

The fact is that the most wine-ignorant person in the room could have done just as well in this blind tasting, up to a point, as our expert. That may come as a surprise. But the truth is that a fresh nose and palate can sometimes do even better than the expert. What novices can't do, of course, is put sensory messages into context. They aren't versed in wine regions and winery styles. And they haven't built up the backlog of experience that is called a "taste memory." The whole performance has been so impressive that it's easy to forget that the wine expert was born ignorant. He almost surely remained ignorant into early adulthood. The body of knowledge he has since accumulated didn't come quickly. And, given the cost of fine wine, it didn't come cheaply. But it did come pleasurably. That same apprenticeship is open to anyone with eyes, nose, and palate—and the will to use them and the intellect together.

Using mouth and mind simultaneously is an alien

practice to most Americans. While the French lovingly perfected the classic meal created by chefs who have undergone an arduous apprenticeship, we perfected fast food prepared primarily by glassy-eyed teenagers working part-time for minimum wage. There's nothing wrong with fast food. But it and the beverages served with it are meant to be grabbed and wolfed down. They are not meant to be focused upon. Indeed, they wouldn't repay that focus. The work day has become so hectic and fast-moving for many people that they may go for days without sitting down to a real meal. In its place is a chain of snacks. Thus a new word, formerly reserved for the dining habits of livestock, has entered the modern American vocabulary: grazing. This lifestyle may mean more output of work, but it also means less input of pleasure.

The sensory aspects of wine are only three: sight, smell, and taste. Each is capable of endless variation. Each refuses to remain static. Each changes as the wine proceeds along its temporal arc, on which the principle points are youth, maturity, and senility. One can venture in many directions and on many byways to learn about wine. But the basis of your knowledge and pleasure will always rest on the triad of sight, smell, and taste.

APPEARANCE

It would seem that not much could be said about the color of wine beyond the obvious: red, white, and rosé. In fact, there is a world of variation in color, hue, and shade. The grape contributes the basic pigments. The winemaker "mixes" them. Age changes them. You can learn much about the type, age, and health of a wine by sight alone. Some of those judgments you'll make will turn out to be wrong, of course. No rule holds absolute in the wine world. But you'll add to your knowledge from the mistakes.

From the gustatory point of view, appearance would seem to be a secondary quality in wine. It's how the wine smells and tastes that counts. Let its looks be damned. But don't be deceived. We place a great deal of emphasis on appearance. The French wine writer Max Leglise tells of an experiment in which three wines—two red and one white—are poured. Expert tasters are blindfolded and asked to pick out the white wine. They were wrong nearly as often as they were right. Leglise also emphasizes the power of color by a single, disquieting suggestion: Imagine that your favorite wine came to the table colored bright blue! You'd probably switch to beer.

Q: *What preliminaries to wine tasting should be observed?*

A: Begin with a clear glass as thin-lipped as possible. (Cut-crystal goblets are fine for water but will block your view of wine.) A tulip- or semi-fishbowl–shaped glass will best hold the smell of the wine. Before you pour, check the inner rim of the newly opened bottle and the surface of the wine to see if any cork particles or other deposits are in sight. If so, wipe away what you can and pour out a bit of wine into a spare glass. The bits of cork should come with it. Now pour some wine into your tasting glass. An ounce or two is plenty. If you will be tasting more than three wines, have a bucket on hand into which you can spit the wine.

Q: *When and how during a tasting does one spit?*

A: If more than three wines are to be tasted, by all means spit. Professionals always do. This means having on hand a nonglass bucket or pitcher (what's in it definitely shouldn't be seen). As for the method of spitting, this is beyond written explanation. My only advice is to pretend you are one of those mini-bellows gadgets from which icing decorations are squeezed onto pastry. I believe the principle of propulsion is identical.

Q: *What is the best light source for wine tasting?*

A: It's not so much the source or wattage of the light as the positioning. Your view of the wine will be most revealing if you tilt the glass down to a white surface with overhead light. That background can be a porcelain sink or plate, or even a clean sheet of paper. If the light source is good, you should see a softly dancing projection of the wine on the white surface.

Q: *What should I look for first?*

A: Clarity. By that, I don't necessarily mean transparency. A young, deeply colored Cabernet Sauvignon or Petite-Syrah will verge on the opaque. But it shouldn't look muddy. Look for those glints as from a gem. If the wine is dull, there are two possibilities. One is faulty winemaking. The other is that the sediment that is natural to many red wines has been roiled as a result of recent jiggling. It can take as long as a day for the sediment to settle back to the bottom of the bottle.

Q: What can be "read" from the color of a red wine?

A: The color of young wine ought to be lively and bright. The exact tint will depend on the skin pigment of the grape type. The darkest, usually, is Petite-Syrah, which veers toward blue-black. It is the only wine that will actually stain a glass. The palest tint is usually Pinot Noir, which often looks like thinned-out cherry or cranberry juice. Cabernet Sauvignon tends to a blend of garnet and purple—or a good ripe plum. The same goes for Zinfandel and Merlot. Gamay tends to a lighter, brighter shade that is closest to strawberry.

As red wine ages, its color will mellow. This is most easily seen at the rim of the glass. In youth, the basic color goes right to the edge. It will lighten, but it won't change color. With age, the rim will gradually turn to a mixture of brown and orange that grows to an ever-paler amber. The center of the glass is where the color will hold most firmly. Even here, it will also lose its fresh, brilliant cherry, garnet, or purple, for a tint that will be closer to mahogany. Though mellow, it won't lack richness.

Q: What is the range of color in white wine?

A: As with red wine, the tint will come from the grape skins, with an additional input from any wood aging the wine might have received. In its youth, white wine will range in color from spring-water clear to buttery yellow. More acidity usually means less color. Sprightly Rieslings, for example, are usually very pale. Rich Chardonnays that have been oak-aged and may be low in acid tend to be the most deeply colored of the dry wines. Sweet wines tend to be yellowest of all.

As white wines age, the process of oxidation in the bottle gradually deepens their color. True white- or green-tinted wines turn light yellow. Wines that were white-yellow turn golden. Sweet wines that were golden may turn, after many years, to the color of caramel—yet still deliver lovely heaps of flavor. Beware of all other white wines, however, once they have edged toward gold. If the wine is Chardonnay, it may well be magnificent still. But it has nowhere to go but downhill. Most other wines will have already made that descent. They may be richly pretty, but they will have become oxidized. This stage is called maderization. The wine will taste like a sherry that has something wrong with it.

Q: *I have occasionally come across colorless hard crystals around the cork of a white wine. What are they?*

A: They are tartrates, or salts of tartaric acid, which precipitate out of the wine when it is chilled. Usually they are eliminated at the winery. However, it's not a sign of sloppy winemaking if they do appear. Filtering out sediments like tartrates also filters out flavor elements, so many winemakers are loath to filter too thoroughly, lest they "strip" the wine. If you find tartrate crystals, there's no need to worry. They are harmless and tasteless. Still, their texture is such that you won't want to drink them. Think of them as you would of bits of shell in a lobster bisque. They are a sign that what you are drinking has been honestly made. Sometimes a retailer will mark down the price of an otherwise superior wine because tartrates are visible. If you like that wine, don't hesitate to buy it.

SMELL

It would be hard to overestimate the influence of smell as a key to our appreciation and identification of wine. Oenologists have gone so far as to suggest that when we taste wine, we are really tasting its smell. There is evidence for this primacy of smell. The co-owner of a Napa Valley winery once told me, for example, of her stint as a judge in a local wine competition at a time she was on a dietary regimen that did not allow her to drink wine. Just the same, she joined the panel of judges. They had before them twelve Cabernet Sauvignons that had reached the finals. While the others tasted each wine, she only sniffed the wines. Yet when the results were compared, her notes showed that she had rated the wines in the same order as the other judges. If this seems like an exceptional feat, it is only because we make the mistake of not giving our olfactory sense its due. According to the great French oenologist Emile Peynaud, our sense of smell is at least ten thousand times sharper than our sense of taste.

Think of how violently we react, to unpleasant smells—a small but overripe fish lying on a dock, for example, or other odors, which needn't be named.

Certain smells can make us sick faster than certain tastes. Even the memory of those smells years later can make us shiver in disgust. Luckily, the reverse is also true. They are as powerfully evocative of days and events past as any material object. Do you remember aromas from childhood of bread baking, of maple syrup being poured on pancakes? Of coffee perking in the kitchen, its aroma seeping into every room of the house? Of certain soaps or of the inimitable fragrance of laundry that's been line-dried in summer sun? Is there any denying that your nose is connected to your memory?

In the here and now of wine evaluation, your nose is both sensor and tool. When you pay careful attention to a wine of distinctive presence, you will discover—or perhaps rediscover—how powerfully discerning is your sense of smell.

Q: Do "raw" grapes and the wine made from them smell the same?

A: They share characteristics in common, but they do not smell the same. Once fermentation has worked its magic on the grape juice, different smells appear. As the wine ages first in cask and then in bottle, other smells take over. In wine terminology, the earlier smell of the new wine is called aroma. As the wine matures in bottle, it achieves bouquet. It is a long distance from the aroma of freshly vinified Cabernet Sauvignon or Pinot Noir to the bouquet of the wine in bottle ten years later. It's that progression that makes wine worth cellaring.

Q: *How can the smells of grape and wine diverge so?*

A: The grape sugars (glucose and fructose) in the mature grape are replaced in wine by ethyl alcohol and a host of flavor compounds. Alcohol seems to magnify smells and carry them to the nose, just as hot cooking oil magnifies and carries the flavor of substances like onion and garlic. What the alcohol carries to your nose are original flavor essences from the grape, along with countless others formed during fermentation. Over forty acids alone have been identified in wine. More flavor changes will occur if a secondary fermentation occurs, in which malic acids are changed to lactic acids, lending a softer, more giving aura to the wine. Yet other smells will emerge if the wine is aged in oak barrels.

Q: *Does wine have a distinct, individual, and unmistakable smell based on the grape from which it was made?*

A: In theory, yes. But there's only one sure way to avoid mistaking a Cabernet Sauvignon for a Pinot Noir, or a Riesling for a Sauvignon Blanc. That's to first catch a glimpse of the label on the bottle. Tasted blind, the various varietal grapes can turn into goblins. They show no respect for professionals in the tricks they love to play. Roy Brady writes, in *The Book of California Wine*, of a blind tasting held by the staff at the esteemed wine research facility at the University of California at Davis. These oneologists had an average of nineteen years' experience. Yet at this tasting they regularly confused one key varietal with another. And these were wines they had made themselves!

You'd have thought that those "pros" could have done better—much better— at identifying the key wines. (They got to taste as well as smell.) But their failure is actually an affirmation of the lively unpredictability of wine. If its identity could be pinned down every time, would it still be worth our enduring interest? We'd get tired of it soon enough.

Q: *Aren't some varietals more easily recognizable than others?*

A: Among the reds, young Zinfandel is usually easiest to pin down, because of its high-profile aroma of berries and peppery spice. As for the whites, Gewürztraminer is also recognizable by its unique aroma of pepper and roses. The hands-down winner in the *vinifera* category, however, is wine made from the Muscat grape. It's hard to say what it smells like. But once met, it's never forgotten. The compound that is responsible for Muscat's uniqueness is called linalool.

Several members of the American family of *labrusca* grapes are the equal of Muscat in assertive aroma. The best known is the Concord. But the most forward is the Niagara grape, which makes a white wine that smells like cheap banana candy. That's not as bizarre as it sounds. Both wine and candy share a flavoring agent called methyl anthranilate.

Q: *What if I just can't smell what others smell in a wine?*

A: Be true to yourself. Every person picks up cer-

tain sensory messages less or more alertly than others
do. You may be highly sensitive to the presence of the
sharp, slightly biting smell called volatile acidity. Another taster may be more attuned to the whiff of sul-
phur dioxide that occasionally comes up from a newly
opened wine. If the smell of a wine reminds you of
something else you know, never be ashamed to say it.
I remember a young woman who was tasting her first
Chardonnay. She repeatedly smelled the wine but refused to offer a word of comment. It would be too
embarrassing, she insisted, to tell what she smelled.
Finally, the word came out: asparagus. She was right,
and several of the more experienced tasters told her
so.

Even wine professionals sometimes hesitate to say
what's truly on their minds in a tasting situation. I
vividly remember just such a situation at a carefully
organized tasting held at Manhattan's International
Wine Center. Two dozen wine experts had before
them a series of four glasses of Pinot Noir made by a
famed California winemaker. One of the wines had
an unusual, even disquieting smell. It was evident
that quite a few tasters were perplexed by it. Yet, with
the winemaker sitting as guest of honor at the head
table, nobody was anxious to say what might have
been on their mind.

Finally, Albert Hotchkin, Jr., director of the center,
cleared his throat. "I know this sounds strange..." he
began. Then he hesitated. Hotchkin was clearly having trouble mustering his courage. Finally, into the
deepening chasm of uncomfortable silence, he said,
"This wine smells like warm Pepsi." And he was
right. I had a sudden flash of myself as a baseball-

loving boy, sitting in the grandstand of long-gone Griffith Stadium in Washington, D.C., sipping Pepsi in a paper cup warmed by a summer's afternoon sun. Now, thirty years later, that precise scent from the paper cup was being invoked from a wine glass. Nowhere in any wine book will you find it written that Pinot Noir can smell like warm Pepsi. And yet there it was, proving two things. The first is that wine will go on surprising you. The second is that while books may guide you, you'd better count on your nose.

Q: *What is the best way to smell a wine?*

A: Put your nose to the rim of the glass and inhale in a few short bursts. That first impression will be your best impression, so give it some thought before you smell again. When you do put your nose to the wine a second time, it should be done to confirm your first impression rather than to find a new one. Too much smelling dulls your nose to a particular scent. We all know what it's like to gradually get used to a smell so that we don't notice it all—even a hospital smell. The same can happen with wine. Your best aid in smelling a wine will be a glass that captures the bouquet or aroma. The tulip shape is ideal.

Q: *Does temperature affect a wine's smell?*

A: The colder the wine, the harder it will be to smell. Let white wines that have been refrigerated warm up in the bottle for ten minutes or so to about 55 or even 60 degrees. That's a bit warmer than you'll want for actual drinking purposes. Red wines reveal their "nose" at room temperature, though they usually taste best at about 65 degrees.

TASTING

Our sense of taste may not be as acute as our sense of smell. But it can do more. Much more. It can deepen and amplify all manner of flavors and nuances picked up by the nose from the bouquet of a mature wine. It can reveal major components of the wine that are off limits to the nose. You can taste but not smell, for example, bitterness. You can't even smell sweetness. If you doubt that, put your nose in the sugar bowl. Where's the sweetness? The many scents of honey come from diverse flowers, not from sugar.

Quite apart from the range of flavors your palate will register from the wine in your mouth, it will reveal the entirely other dimension called "structure." This is one of prime mystery words of the wine cult. Sentences and bridges have structure, but how can a liquid have it? And yet, as poorly evocative as the word is, wines worth your contemplation do have a structure. What is most surprising and even miraculous about that structure is it relates not to engineering but to traits of human character. More about that will be said below.

Q: What does one actually taste in a wine?

A: D. Maynard Amerine, dean of American oenologists, puts it in a nutshell: "Wine is a chemical symphony composed of ethyl alcohol, several other alcohols, sugars, other carbohydrates, polyphenols, aldehydes, ketones, enzymes, pigments, at least half a dozen vitamins, 15 to 20 minerals, more than twenty-two organic acids, and other grace notes that have not yet been identified."

In simpler terms, remember that the tongue only picks up four classes of tastes: sweet, sour, bitter, and salty. Since wines aren't salty, that leaves only three to consider.

What you are tasting for, then, is a balance among fruit (which is the same as flavor), acids, and alcohol. The most straightforward case would be a fruity, slightly sweet white wine, like Riesling. The wine has a vigorous, direct fruitiness, which must be balanced by the right degree of acidity. If the acidity is too low, the wine will be merely sweet and cloying. The taste won't have any of the liveliness that acid gives. Have you ever tasted a fresh apricot that had delicious, mild flavor but no zip? That's due to a lack of acidity, which is common to apricots. If you make a fruit ice out of apricots, you'll also find that it is rather "flat." Lemon ice, on the other hand, always has a refreshing zing—even though its flavor is not nearly so rich as that of a fruit like apricot. Lots of sugar has to be added, of course, to put all that acid in balance.

When a wine goes over to the side of being too acidic, it tastes tart, or "bitey." The fresh-fruit comparison, in this case, would be to a pineapple. That fruit can be simultaneously quite sweet and flavorful and yet too acidic. It stings your mouth. If, however, you put a slice of that pineapple on a piece of bread, or plain pound cake, it will be more pleasing to the taste, because the acidity has been buffered without blocking that lovely pineapple flavor. Put a dab of whipped cream on a bite of pineapple and the acidity will also be softened. In short, a white wine succeeds when fruit and acid are in balance. Even a very sweet, "Sauternes"-style wine must have that fruit/acid balance, or it will taste more like pancake syrup than wine.

Q: Does that fruit/acid balance also hold for red wines?

A: It is more subtle, since a fine red wine has more flavor shadings than a simple white wine. And a third element is also introduced to the critical balance: the bitterness of tannins. They come from the grape skins, pits, and stems that churn with the juice during fermentation and, later, from the oak barrels in which the wine ages. Early in the life of the wine, the bitterness of those tannins creates a major imbalance in its taste. Tannic acid is the same compound that "tans" leather. You will feel the burn of those tannins not on your tongue but on your gums. The feeling will persist long after the wine has left your mouth. The assault of "big" tannins will ruin the pleasure of a young wine.

Q: Why can't red wine tannins be restrained?

A: That would be like cutting out the wine's backbone. Tannins keep the wine firm as it ages. Slowly, they soften as the flavors of the wine amplify. Eventually, tannins and flavor come into perfect balance. A wine at the same age without tannic support will have weakened to the point where it provides no pleasure.

Q: *I like my red wine to be dry. But sometimes the taste goes beyond dry to tart. Am I supposed to appreciate tartness?*

A: You aren't "supposed" to appreciate a tart wine or any other. Appreciation must come voluntarily or not at all. As to your specific question: Tartness comes from high acidity. As long as the acids in the wine are balanced by the weight of full flavor, all is well. But underripe grapes can push that balance the wrong way. And some acids are more "tart" than others. Malic acids (as in a sour apple), for example, are sharp, while lactic acid (as in milk) is mellower. That is why a winemaker may induce a secondary, or "malolactic," fermentation to convert the harder acid to the softer, with an accompanying mellowing of the wine. It's important not to jump to a conclusion that a wine is too tart. For one thing, the palate is most sensitive to acids at first taste. And don't forget that red wine is made to be drunk with foods that will be complemented by a certain tartness in the wine.

Q: *Do tannins contribute to tartness?*

A: No. Tannins contribute to astringency—which is not the same as tartness. (Only acidity causes tartness.) A young, very ripe wine could be low in malic acidity and yet be loaded with mouth-puckering tannins. It isn't so hard as you might think to discriminate between acidity and astringency. Just remember that you'll feel the sharp blade of acidity as soon as you taste, while the bitterness will come on last. When a wine is described as having a lingering bitter aftertaste, be assured that is the tannins "kicking in" late. Think of how long it takes for the effects of chili peppers to be felt. "This isn't so hot," you'll say of chili or of an Indian vindaloo. And then, very slowly, the burn will begin. By then it's too late. Even water won't help.

Q: *What is meant by a wine's "structure"?*

A: When the diverse elements of a wine are in balance, you will feel that harmony in the mouth. That feeling is expressed as structure. It won't do for the wine to be merely flavorful. It must have the underlying acidity and tannic backbone to support that flavor. In a wine of superior structure, you will experience a sort of swelling chord of flavor, which then diminishes very slowly to a whisper. That first taste is called the "attack." It shouldn't reveal all that the wine has to give. The flavor should expand in your mouth. This is sometimes called the "middle taste." Then the taste diminishes. This is known as the wine's "finish," and the longer, the better.

Q: *Does any one factor separate great wines from merely very good ones?*

A: It's the finish that tells the story of ultimate quality. A very good wine may have a beautiful "attack." It may fill your mouth with flavor of the most exquisite quality. But if that flavor dies on you too quickly, then the wine remains what it started out to be—very good. Great wines must have that finish which lasts and lasts. At the very end, you won't know whether the presence of that wine still caresses your palate or has slipped into your memory. Years later, you may have forgotten what you ate, and even who you sat at table with. But you won't have forgotten what was in your glass. Even your glass doesn't forget. Once the last drop of great is gone, the scent of that wine will remain in the glass for several moments.

Q: *What are some tasting comparisons that will help to sharpen my sense?*

A: It doesn't matter whether you start with red or white. But do compare wines made from the same grape. My suggestion is to start with wines of the same vintage as well—but from different areas. This is a "horizontal" tasting. You have the best chance to see the most dramatic differences if you compare, say, a Cabernet from Mendocino ("North Coast") with one from Monterey ("Central Coast"). If you can get hold of an East Coast version, that will make for a third, very distinctive personality.

Next time, try three or more wines of the same grape from different vintages—a "vertical" tasting. Ideally, they should be from the same winery, or at least from the same viticultural area. It won't always be easy to find bottles for a vertical tasting. It will probably be easiest to seek out various vintages of a major winery like Robert Mondavi, Beaulieu, or Inglenook. It doesn't matter in which order you taste, though I'd put the oldest and youngest wines side by side to maximize the contrast. It will be quite exciting when you are suddenly struck by the difference between the berryish, oaky aroma of a young "Cab" and the more harmonious, deeper bouquet of a mature bottle.

In setting up the tasting, it's best if you can line up a glass for each wine, side by side. This will give you instant access to color comparisons. Pour a few ounces in each glass just before the tasting begins. Your reactions will be most unvarnished if you keep the bottles out of sight until all wines have been tasted. And, by all means, smell all the wines before tasting any of them. Then you will learn if your taste confirms your nose. Usually, it will. Take notes immediately after tasting each wine. Be brief but do cover these points: What is the color? How does it smell (fruit, spice, oak?)? Is the taste soft or harsh, lean or full? Does the flavor remind you of anything (mushrooms, cherries, mint?)? Does the flavor linger long, or does it stop short? Finally, remember to spit, or you may discover in the morning that the more you sipped, the more your penmanship deteriorated.

BUBBLES

I T is the French who invented sparkling wine, in the eighteenth century. It is they who perfected this most civilized of liquids. And it is they who, after a great deal of serious practice, still know best how to enjoy it. We Americans tend to limit our own enjoyment of the foil-necked bottles to birthdays, weddings, graduations, and other occasions requiring all hands to raise a glass in toast. The French know, however, that sparkling wine is unique in its ability to lend pleasure to a much wider array of occasions. Being a people who are intolerant of dreariness, the French are particularly alert to the need, from time to unpredictable time, to dust off the slender glasses, drop a tray of ice into the silvery cooler, and plunge in a bottle of "bubbly" for no other reason than to freshen up an hour of life when nothing is happening at all.

The essence of the French attitude toward sparkling wine was made clear to me one Sunday morning as I entered the bar car of the Paris–Bordeaux express train. I had a cup of coffee in mind—the only beverage I was accustomed to at mid-morning. But then I saw, seated at a banquette table, a girl of about fourteen years old who was seated beside a dark-suited, dignified, even severe old man of about eighty —clearly her grandfather. Between them was one of those handsome stainless-steel commercial wine buckets whose streamlined design seems to have been fixed back in the 1930s. The conversation of this pair of travelers was spirited—helped along, no doubt, by what they were sipping. For that young girl, holding that glass of champagne as an adjunct to conversation already seemed to come as naturally to her as it did to the old man.

Had I been more flexible, I'd have taken a cue from that odd couple and switched from coffee—not my first cup of the morning—to a split of champagne. But though I was tempted, obstinacy of American custom took charge. Instead of enjoying those bubbles, lovely even in a clear plastic flute, I sprinkled the contents of an instant coffee packet into a cup of hot water. And all because the clock said 10:45 A.M. But that morning, a seed was planted. I've since learned how much more pleasing a sparkling wine is to the eye and palate than is a mid-morning cup of coffee that, as often as not, has turned nasty from too long a stint on the heat. I try to make sure I'm not wrong about this at least once a month. So far the bubbles have made their point every time.

A BRIEF EXPLANATION OF HOW BUBBLES GET INTO THE BOTTLE

Unlike still wines, the best of which are vinified with a maximum of care but a minimum of fuss, sparkling wine is always the result of an elaborate intervention by the maker. The cult of minimal treatment, practiced by so many small wineries, simply will not do when it comes to sparkling wines. The first champagne maker is said to have been the Benedictine monk Dom Perignon, who lived in the Champagne region, located 120 miles east of Paris. As with other enormously important or popular inventions (penicillin, Silly Putty, etc.), in this case the monk is said to have stumbled on the process by accident in the cellar of his abbey. His cry of astonishment at his own first sip—"I have tasted the stars!"—is still the most concise and evocative definition of sparkling wine. What lends special poignancy to that cry is that Dom Perignon, we are told, was blind.

The *methode champenoise*, begun by Dom Perignon and elaborated over three centuries by his followers, begins with the picking of the grapes while they're still unripe—that is, high in acids and low in sugar. These grapes would pucker your mouth. Sugar will be added later to correct the balance, but acid can't be legally added. And it is acid that will be the backbone of the wine. Most sparkling wines are a blend of several grape varieties. Champagne and wines in its tradition usually contain Chardonnay, Pinot Noir, and Pinot Blanc. At the winery, each batch of grapes is separately handled and vinified like any other still wine. By spring, the different wines are ready—though they remain nastily, undrinkably acidic. But the winemaker perceives in each of them the essential qualities that will contribute to the final blend. The Chardonnay, for example, will provide complexity, the Pinot Noir smoothness, and the Pinot Blanc verve.

The blended wine now goes into the bottle. You may have noticed that sparkling wine bottles are heavier than normal bottles. This is so that the bottles can withstand the pressures built up during fermentation. Each bottle is filled only about four-fifths full. The empty space is then filled with the all-important *dosage*—a solution of sugar and fresh yeasts. The bottle is then temporarily sealed, usually with a cork-lined metal cap. The wine is then cellared. For several months the yeasts, doing what they do best, feed on the sugar. The by-products of this meal, as in the still wine process, are alcohol and carbon dioxide. But the CO_2, which escapes into the air during normal fermentation in open vats, remains locked in the bottle. Hence, the bubbles.

As with any other fermentation, this one, carried out in the bottle, leaves behind a residue of dead yeasts, which must be removed. Enter now the specialist known as the *remueur*, or "riddler." Daily, he gives each downward-tilted bottle a quick twist. That action nudges the residue down toward the mouth of the bottle. After a few weeks of riddling, all the solids have lodged against the cap. Now the neck of the bottle is frozen in a brine solution. When the cap is pulled off, pressure built up within the bottle—about 90 pounds per square inch—forces out the ice capsule in the neck. In goes a *dosage* of more sparkling wine, mixed with a bit of sugar. The winemaker may also choose to add a splash of brandy, giving an extra flavor impact to the final blend. All these steps are done quickly, so that the loss of precious bubbles is minimized.

The bottle is now sealed with the familiar mushroom-shaped cork. Since corks have been known to take unguided flights under conditions of excessive heat or movement, the wire muzzle tightened over the cork is not merely for show. And, except for the labeling and foil wrap, that's it. Though the new wine will rest now for a period of several months to several years, it is ready to be drunk from this moment on. Time may bring certain nuances to sparkling wine, but it will never undergo the dramatic development of flavor in bottle that is expected of the finest red and white still wines.

Q: *Can the* methode champenoise *be cut short?*

A: It can and is. The method closest to the original is called the "transfer method." It starts out exactly like the traditional method, with fermentation of the young blended wine in bottle under a temporary cap. But at this point, the labor-intensive riddling process is eliminated in favor of pouring the wine from all the bottles into a single pressurized vat. Their accumulated residues settle to the bottom of the vat, where they are drawn off with a minimum of effort. A single *dosage* can now be added at once. The wine is then rebottled, corked, and labeled.

Here in America the transfer method has a payoff that goes well beyond the enormous savings in labor. It makes possible these government-authorized words on the label: "Fermented in the bottle." To consumers who have only the vaguest notion of how sparkling wine is made, the implication of these words is that the wine has been made according to the hand-tailored standard of real champagne. But wines actually made by the *methode champenoise* can use, in addition to that term itself, a slightly different wording on the label: "Fermented in *this* bottle." That small prepositional switch between "the" and "this" hides a major difference in how the bubbles got into the bottle.

Q: *Are there any further shortcuts beyond the transfer method?*

A: The French would prefer to pin the invention of the ultimate shortcut in making sparkling wine on a foreigner—preferably an American. But it was the work of one of their own. His name was Henri Charmat. His method, introduced about 1906, eliminates bottle fermentation altogether. The entire process is carried out in big vats. Only after the *dosage* has been added is the wine bottled. American sparkling wines using this process must use one of two terms on the label: "Bulk process" or "Charmat process." The biggest user of this process in the world is Gallo. It produces nearly 100 million bottles yearly, most of them under the Andre trademark. The label says "Charmat process"—immortalizing a man unknown to any but a tiny fraction of drinkers.

Yet another French innovation—this one involving method champenoise itself—is being tested by the august champagne firm of Möet et Chandon. The yeasts which traditionally float free in the bottle have been encased into dark little beads which have been likened to caviar eggs. Actually, they are more like nets (made of a natural substance called calcium alginate) which allow the yeasts to ferment the wine unhindered. Instead of having to be coached to the neck of the bottle by frequent riddling, however, the beads promptly sink from their own weight once fermentation is complete. They can then be much more easily removed than the traditional yeast sediment.

Q: *Can one tell from the label how dry a sparkling wine will be?*

A: In a bow to the originators, most sparkling wine makers worldwide use French nomenclature to indicate the relative dryness of what is in the bottle. *Nature* is dryest of the dry. It means, at least in theory, that no sugar *dosage* was added to the final blend. Most Americans (but fewer Frenchmen) would find a wine this dry verging on medicinal. *Brut* is next-driest. Then comes an American term, "Extra Dry," which in fact is likely to be slightly off-dry. You can be almost certain that a sparkler marked *Sec* will be sweet. *Demi-sec* will be the sweetest of all. This system is not entirely logical, but then logic is not the priority in the matter of sparkling wine.

Q: *What do the label terms* Blanc de Blanc *and* Blanc de Noirs *mean?*

A: They indicate that the wine is not a blend of both red and white grapes, as in the basic tradition of champagne, but is vinified only from one or the other. *Blanc de blanc* means that only white wine grapes are used. Sometimes it will be just one grape, like Chardonnay or Riesling. *Blanc de noirs* is usually made from the Pinot Noir. Since we know that the juice of almost all "black" grapes is actually white, its quick separation from the color-producing skins immediately upon pressing will leave the juice clear. A slight bit of skin contact will produce the violet or coral tint of "pink champagne."

Q: *Are single-grape sparkling wines better than blends?*

A: Their premium price—particularly in the case of a "blanc de Chardonnay"—would lead you to believe that they are better. But I believe you'll find that blends are more satisfying even as they are less expensive. Take care to find a blend that suits your preference for a sparkling wine that is light or full-bodied, dry or fruity. Single grapes shine best as still wines. The one blanc de blanc that stands apart, incidentally, is made from Muscat grapes. Even the elaborate process of making sparkling wine cannot tame its ripe and inimitably enticing flavor. Muscat is an unstoppable grape. Refined tastes will turn away from it—as do nearly all domestic sparkling winemakers. If you should come across a good Italian or French version, my suggestion is that you suspend refinement of taste for as long as it takes to sip through a bottle.

Q: *Where did the American sparkling wine industry begin?*

A: Not where you'd expect: Within the city limits of Cincinnati, Ohio. Sparkling wine was first made there in 1842, from the Catawba grape, by a pint-sized entrepreneur named Nicholas Longworth. The *Illustrated London News* reported in 1858 that the

"Sparkling Catawba," as Longworth named it, "transcends the Champagne of France." By 1860, Longworth's vines were dying of the then untreatable disease called odium. The local wine industry never revived. But other sparkling wines were coming out of California and New York. French techniques weren't easily learned. Bottles exploded and wines went flat. Most early makers failed. Three from California that endured were Almaden, Korbel, and Paul Masson—all founded between 1876 and 1884. Sparkling wine was one of the few vinous enterprises in which California lagged in prestige behind New York. The legend goes that a taster exclaimed, upon sampling a New York sparkling wine blended from Catawba and Delaware grapes, "Truly, this will be the great champagne of the West!" By the "West," he meant the whole continent. And so "Great Western" got its name. Made at Hammondsport on Keuka Lake in the Finger Lakes district, it was, among a number of notable examples, the nation's most popular sparkling wine until the onset of Prohibition.

Q: And what about sparkling wine in our own times?

A: Sparkling wine excitement didn't really arise again in America until 1973, when the illustrious French firm of Moët et Chandon established Domaine Chandon in the heart of the Napa Valley. The French firm had chosen the right moment to arrive. Napa Valley wines of that year would score astonishing successes in Steven Spurrier's Paris tasting three years later. Fine wine, whether still or sparkling, suddenly seemed immensely exciting to a rising number of Americans just awakening to the pleasures of the table.

The success of Domaine Chandon, whose production increased geometrically during the 1970s, seems to have ignited interest from far and near in making sparkling wine in the French tradition. Another major French firm, Piper-Heidsieck, soon established the Piper-Sonoma label in partnership with Sonoma Vineyards. The century-old Spanish firm of Freixnet has also began making a sparkler called Gloria Ferrer in Sonoma. From the home ground, Chateau Saint Jean, Sonoma's premier white wine house, introduced its new sparkling wine in 1984. Other new entries include Sebastiani, Iron Horse, and Robert Hunter. They join a few established makers of premium sparkling wine ranging from tiny, upper-end Schramsberg to Korbel, which in 1985 surpassed 1 million cases and is currently the largest adherent to *methode champenoise*. Korbel actually invented, twenty years ago, a riddling machine to automate the most labor-intensive phase of the process. In 1985, about 4 million cases of sparkling wine were made by the *methode champenoise*—up from fewer than a million cases just a decade earlier.

Q: *Will the differences in taste among cheap, moderate, and high priced sparkling wine be obvious to me?*

A: Sparkling wines don't betray their price categories as strikingly as still wines. A buttery-textured, oak-aged Chardonnay, for example, will never be mistaken for a budget bottle of white table wine. Neither will a deep-flavored Cabernet Sauvignon be mistaken for jug red wine. In these still wines, the quality of the grape shines through quite directly. But the sparkling-wine maker can "play around" in ways that are off limits to the still winemaker. He can alter the blend of grapes at will, add sugar to taste, as well as that splash of brandy just before corking. In his non-vintage wine, he will also use vats from different years. The winemaker's prerogative, in short, is to act like a skilled chef who can turn the ingredients at hand into a pleasing mouthful—as when cheap cuts of meat are turned into a flavorful stew.

A case in point is the sparkling wine made in New York State and Ohio from native American grapes like Catawba, Niagra and Delaware. As still wines, these grapes may seem, to our "French grape" palate, rather too grapey and one-dimensional. But under the hand of the master blender, their taste becomes less blatant—or, to put it positively, more subtle. Properly iced and served in correct glassware, even the chea-pest sparkler can be mistaken for much more expen-sive stuff. This can be embarrassing more to the server than the served, as I discovered one New Year's Eve when my guests sipped an "American Champagne" called Gold Medal Brut from bottles they could not see. It was made in Batavia, New York, and it cost an incredible $2.99. One guest who knows and appreciates good wine took a sip and made the face she normally reserves for real champagne.

"This is wonderful!" she said. But when she asked which "champagne" it was, I volunteered only that it was the "Special Reserve of the House."

Q: *Are you giving the back of your hand to the higher priced sparkling wines?*

A: My praise of the best examples of low-priced wines isn't meant to belittle luxury-class versions—whether it be real champagne or wines made by its methods. A high standard of grape selection and of winemaking will show up in the bottle. As with the finest still wines, you'll mark it by a firm concentration of flavor and, above all, an intense and lingering aftertaste. The truest test of a sparkling wine's breeding is to let a glass go flat and warm. This makes it, as it were, "naked," with all assets and defects revealed. Now taste it. You should discern what you did before —a wine of firm flavor concentration with an intense and lingering aftertaste. Frankly, don't expect a cheap sparkler to hold up well under this same test. It will likely be sweetly insipid. The aftertaste won't linger long, if it exists at all, and that's probably just as well.

If a winemaker has taken pains to produce the best possible sparkling wine, then it deserves your attention and even your contemplation. Otherwise, his or her efforts and your dollars are wasted. So I'd strongly suggest that such a wine not be served when the focus of attention is elsewhere. When you are raising your glass to your horse that has just won the Kentucky Derby, for example, do it with the cheap stuff. Save the best for sipping in intimate company at an hour that is serene.

Q: *Do the bubbles themselves—size or number—tell anything about the quality of a sparkling wine?*

A: You will hear it said that the bubbles are smallest and persist longest in the best wines. It's not necessarily true. The bubble "quotient" is a function of how much extra yeast and juice went into the second fermentation. The more extra fermentation, the more bubbles. That doesn't make it a better wine. Too much carbonation, in fact, can turn the wine aggressive, so that it is almost stinging to the mouth. As for the persistence of the bubbles, this is most dependent on temperature (the colder the better) and shape of the glass.

Q: *Does sparkling wine require a special glass?*

A: In theory, a wine ought to taste the same in a jelly jar as in the most exquisite, thin-lipped, full-leaded crystal ware. But fine wine doesn't respond to that theory. In the case of sparkling wines, suitable glassware is keyed to function as well as to aesthetics. A tall, slender glass will best show off the bubbles. It will also minimize the liquid's contact with air, so that the bubbles tend to dissipate less quickly. Wide- and shallow-bowled glasses of the old style, so emblematic of glamorous evenings on luxury liners of half a century ago, do just the opposite. They don't give the bubbles much depth from which to travel upward but do allow them to be expended quickly. By all means, invest in a half dozen champagne glasses. They can be straight-sided "flutes" or contoured like an elongated tulip. As with other wine glasses, they should be clear, and thin of lip.

Since sparkling wine does have an aura of luxury to it, don't hesitate to invest in an ice bucket of a design that pleases you—preferably one with a floor stand. You can then station it where apéritifs are being served or beside the dining table. You will probably use it more frequently for still wine than sparkling wine.

Q: *How long does it take to cool down a bottle of sparkling wine from room temperature?*

A: About ninety minutes in the refrigerator, forty-five minutes in the freezer compartment, and twenty minutes in an icewater-filled bucket. Chill the wine in the neck of the bottle by turning it upside down in the bucket for the last five minutes.

Q: *Are you a proponent of the "champagne brunch?"*

A: I am. Apart from the special aura a sparkling wine lends to brunch—and I'm talking about one that starts, or at least begins, in the A.M. rather than the P.M.—it also complements, as no other wine can, the basic brunch standbys: omelets, bacon, ham, and even smoked salmon—a food that turns most other wines "fishy." It's often said, incidentally, that sparkling wine shows its best with salty foods. All those brunch foods just mentioned fall into that category.

Q: *Any thoughts about mimosas for brunch?*

A: Plain orange juice, even if fresh-squeezed, is too sweet to start off the proceedings. It is much improved when it is mixed with an equal amount of sparkling wine, which perks the appetite very well. If you're the preparer, however, this is another instance when you don't really want to waste a best bottle on the mixture. Its subtle qualities will be lost.

Q: *What else profits from being mixed with sparkling wine?*

A: A "kir"—white wine with a touch of cassis syrup—is a lovely cocktail drink that is even more vivacious when made with "bubbly." A few ripe raspberries, lightly crushed, can also be an exquisite addition to a glass of sparkling wine at either end of any meal.

Q: *Does it ever make sense to serve sparkling wine all through dinner?*

A: Even the finest sparkling wine can turn into too much of a good thing. It's better to exercise restraint and limit it to the apéritif hour and then, possibly, continue serving it with a first course tailored to it (the French would elect for *foie gras*—duck liver.) and then on to other wines. The exception—there always is one with wine—would come when you want to put the spotlight on a particularly prized bottle of red wine. Then you would serve a sparkler throughout the meal, from which red meat has been banished—right up to a carefully chosen cheese course. That regimen of sparkling wine will have left your palate not only surprisingly fresh but primed for the red wine experience. It had better be a bottle worth this rather exceptional build-up.

Q: *Any last word on ultimate marriages of sparkling wine and food?*

A: Freshly popped and buttered popcorn is too good to be downed with soft drinks. Try it with sparkling wine of as fine a quality as you dare. I know this sounds silly, but it works.

DEALING
WITH
YOUR
WINE
SHOP

Q: How can I tell if a wine shop is good?

A: I'll answer by focusing, all through this chapter, on a single shop. It's not perfect. It sometimes gets undersold by other shops. But it's an honorable place where pains are taken to select and care for wine with respect—and only then to sell it. The shop is called Town Wine & Spirits. It's located in unsung little Rumford, Rhode Island, four hours of turnpike driving away from my own Manhattan home.

It was just before Easter, some ten years ago, when I came across a wine ad for Town in the Providence *Journal*. An array of impressive, even classic wines was offered with prices to match. It seemed unlikely, frankly, that such wines were being offered in a place that I, a proud Manhattanite, had never heard of. I didn't gain a better opinion as I came upon the store itself, on dreary Newport Avenue. With its charmless facade and flat roof and its front window stacked with cases of beer, Town Liquor as it was then called, appeared to be no different from numberless other booze and beer shops far from fine wine country.

It seemed as if this would turn out to be a wasted

trip—until I noticed, attached to the rear of the store, a two-level, windowless brick cube all abristle with air conditioning vents. Ugly as the cube was, I knew instantly that it set Town apart from all but a very few wine shops. It could only be an above-ground "cave" where wines slumbered at constant temperature from one season into the next.

Q: *So the key word is "storage"?*

A: Proper storage is certainly first on our list of attributes required of a serious wine store. Both red and white wines can be harmed by warm or unstable temperatures. Just how much harm is tricky to measure. Rarely is a wine totally spoiled unless it is baked. More often, it merely loses its more chipper qualities, like someone who is visibly a bit wilted at the end of too hot a day. At a constant temperature of about 55 degrees, however, wine's vitality will be preserved for many years. Most wine shops do not have access to a natural cellar that maintains those cool temperatures. So, as at Town, one must be built. It doesn't come cheap. After initial construction costs come hefty electric bills, especially in summer months. If the proprietor charges a bit more for a particular bottle than a competitor who takes no special pains with storage, he deserves every penny of it.

Q: *But storage is for the long haul. Don't wine stores turn over their stock fast enough to make elaborate storage facilities unnecessary?*

A: Gallo and other "bread and butter" wines had *better* turn over fast, or most wine shops would soon be out of business. But hundreds of other wines—

those that make a wine buff's heart thump faster—
may be on hand for years. That's how stock is built
"in depth." And those are the wines that must be
stored properly. A wine shop is not like a retailer of
fashion. The longer the merchandise is on hand, the
more valuable it becomes.

Q: *Should one ask where a shop keeps its wines?*

A: That's a silly question when buying Hearty Burgundy—and an essential one when the bottle on the
counter is a five-year-old Chardonnay or a decade-old
Pinot Noir. Well stored, the wine could be at its peak
of flavor. Parked in the sun or, even worse, next to a
hot water pipe, it could be in decline.

Q: *The 55-degree "windowless brick cube" may be a
great environment for the wine within. But what
about the wine that's out front on the display shelf?*

A: The display wine will certainly not thrive as the
stored wine. And that's why I was both impressed and
pleased to see, when I first entered Town, only one
bottle of each wine on display. That meant that all the
rest of the stock was back in the cube, where it be-
longed. Most proprietors are hesitant to do this, since
unless the selection is vast, the single-bottle display
can give an impression of scarcity to the shelves.

Q: *Is there a right way for wines to be displayed?*

A: There's a logical way. French wines will be
grouped according to place or origin. As the Bordeaux
commune of Margaux is next to that of Saint-Julien
is next to that of Pauillac is next to that of Saint-
Estèphe, so their wines should be arranged on the

display shelf. Rhône wines should be divided between those from the north and those from the south of the region. The brown-tinted bottles identifying German wines of the Rhine ought to be separate from the green-tinted bottles from the Moselle.

Since American wines lack meaningful appellations, however, it is more sensible to group them by state of origin and then by varietal type. You should be able to inspect, say, all California Chardonnays or Zinfandels without wondering whether you are missing any. Ideally, the wines will be alphabetized by winery name within each varietal type so that you can quickly locate Acacia, Alexander Valley or Almadén Chardonnays at one end of the racks and ZD or Zaca Mesa at the other. There should be a rack of oversized bottles for big dinners and—even more useful—a selection of half bottles for when the meal is for two only, or even for one.

Q: *Should bottles be displayed upright or on their sides?*

A: Wines in long-term storage must be stored on their sides. That keeps the cork wet and swelled up to make a tight fit at the neck of the bottle. If the bottle is upright, the cork will dry out, ever so slowly. A dry cork is a shrunken cork. Air can then seep into the bottle and ruin the wine. The difference between a dry and wet cork is easy to demonstrate. Just try to put a cork back in a bottle that's been on its side. The wet end won't go in, but the dry end will.

But don't automatically downgrade a wine shop that displays its bottles upright. It takes months for a cork to dry out (an interval that would be much shorter if not for the lead foil or plastic wrapper over the cork). Most display wines are moved in that time.

Q: *Can you tell if a wine is spoiled by looking into the bottle?*

A: Certain signs ought to make you suspicious. A poor fill level means either that the bottle was not properly filled at the winery or that a bad cork is allowing wine to evaporate. Forget that bottle. Be wary of red wines that have a pale, watery aspect when held up to the light. This is easiest to see in the neck of the bottle. Take the opposite tack with white wines. An amber or deep golden tint suggests that the wine is going or gone. (The exception is fine sweet wines, which can be expected to darken with age.)

Since most wine bottles are tinted green or brown, it's difficult to make absolute judgments of color. A very few wine stores (Town included) provide for their customers a naked, clear, and quite powerful light bulb for checking the color of wine in the bottle. Even with this aid, color can't be considered an absolute measure of the flavor of wine. Old Pinot Noirs, in particular, can be nearly as pale as rosé yet still fill your mouth with rich, round flavors. We talked in more detail about wine color in chapter 4. Here, it is enough to say that any shop that bothers with the minor luxury of a naked bulb for its customers is a very thoughtful shop indeed.

Q: *Are there any other quality checks on a wine shop's stock?*

A: The wine manager at Town, a young fanatic named Nick Zeiser, suggests this quick check of how well a wine shop is stocked: "Look at the vintage dates of white wines meant to be drunk as young as possible. That would mean the Italian Soaves, the French Muscadets, and especially the American white wines made from grapes that normally make red wine—white Zinfandel, for example. These wines lose their freshness quickly. If they're more than two years old, they're tired. Any store that keeps them in regular stock is not on its toes. They should be in the bargain basket."

Zeiser is not, obviously, talking about the few varietal white wines that can gain deeper character and extra flavor nuances with age. Among American wines, this category is limited to fine Chardonnay, Pinot Blanc, and late-harvest sweet wines. One of the pleasures of a well-stocked wine shop is to find one of these wines that you can take charge of once the shop has nursed it through adolescence.

Q: *What about sales help?*
A: A fine wine shop without a knowledgeable salesperson on the floor would be like a garage without a mechanic on duty. My definition of the ideal salesperson is arbitrary: he or she is a person who awakes in the morning and immediately begins to think about what wine to drink with dinner. Zeiser of Town, for example, tied for second in the prestigious and difficult "Wine Wizard" competition for 1986. Even the salesperson who takes home a different bottle each day, however, can't be expected to sample more than a fraction of an ever-changing stock of hundreds of wines. So don't take it as a sign of ignorance if the salesperson is candid enough to admit

that he or she hasn't sampled a wine you've asked about.

What the salesperson can be expected to comment on is the style of the winery in question—whether, for example, the Cabernet Sauvignons are vinified for early drinking or else are tannic and need years of bottle aging. He will know if the winemaker favors a Chardonnay that is voluptuously ripe and soft, in the traditional style of California, or less overtly fruity and more acidic, in the French manner. It is too much to ask of any salesperson to keep track of more than a fraction of the best American wines. Since he's constantly comparing notes with other wine enthusiasts, however, chances are that he's heard an opinion about the wine which interests you.

Q: *Are there particular questions a novice should ask a salesperson?*

A: First comes the particular questions the salesperson should ask *you*. They should be, roughly, as follows:

—Are you looking for a wine for your table or as a gift for another?
—If it is for your table, is the wine to be used as an apéritif or with the meal? What food must the wine accompany? For how many people?
—What style of wine do you prefer? Dryer or with a bit of sweetness? Full-flavored or delicate? (What customers say they like can be at odds with what they actually prefer. A dictum of the wine trade is that we Americans "think dry but drink sweet." The best way to get at

the truth is for the salesperson to ask what particular wine the customer has liked in the past. Its characteristics may well differ from those that have been declared as a preference.)

—Once the salesperson has gathered the answers to the above questions, he or she can ask the essential and final question: How much do you wish to spend?

Q: *But that's the problem. How much must I spend to get quality wine?*

A: Nothing else we eat or drink varies so widely—and sometimes so preposterously—in price as wines made from identical varieties of the grape. I remember the comment a famous restaurateur made about twenty years ago, that no bottle of wine ought to cost more than ten dollars. Despite the intervening inflation, a corollary to that dictim is still true: You need never spend more than ten dollars to buy a fine bottle of American wine. On the other hand, don't expect to pay less than five dollars. Your salesperson should have no trouble providing you with many choices within this range.

Q: *Sometimes a salesperson will try to talk me out of buying a favorite wine. Should I stick to my guns?*

A: A good salesperson, insists Zeiser of Town, is correct not to always let you buy what you want—especially if it's the same bottle that you bought last time. "People latch on to the first wine they discover they like," he explains. "And they end up never trying anything else. They're afraid they'll be disappointed. But the fun of wine is that there's always a new bottle to love—if only you'll have the courage to try it. It gives me a good feeling to move a customer up to a wine that is a bit more subtle, more 'advanced,' each time he or she comes into the store." If necessary, Zeiser admits, he'll even hide the customer's previous wine when he sees him or her arriving. Then, with a straight face, he explains that the store is sold out of the wine the customer liked so much. "It may be a lie," says Zeiser, "but I'm trying to widen that customer's horizons."

Q: *Should I be offended when the salesperson suggests a wine for more than I told him I want to spend?*
A: No salesperson has a right to suggest a wine significantly more expensive than the budget you have set. The issue isn't whether you can afford it. It's whether the salesperson is going to do what you want or what he wants. An incident sticks in my mind, or I should say my craw: I'd asked for a well-rated Gewürztraminer in a Manhattan wine shop. It was priced at seven dollars. "That wine's out of stock," said the too cheerful salesman. "But here's another 'Gewürz' I highly recommend."

I don't doubt that his recommendation was a good one. But at eleven dollars, it cost more than half as much again as the wine I'd asked for. I've seen that salesman many times in the years since he proposed that wine—which in a situation of my own choosing I'd have been more than willing to buy. He knows that I don't care to deal with him, although he probably doesn't know why. For his own sake, I hope that he's learned not to counter-propose wines much more expensive than his customers ask for.

Q: *Is there any reason not to buy a wine I like by the case?*

A: Try to resist. As it is, there are far too many interesting wines to try and not enough occasions to go at it. You'll also find that if you love a particular wine, you'll value it even more if you own fewer bottles of it. Six bottles of any one wine should suffice. If you restrain the admittedly powerful impulse to snap up a case of wines you admire, you'll have more room both in your cellar and on your table for all those other wines you keep meaning to try. Wouldn't you really rather have the experience of sipping six different Cabernet Sauvignons, each of which pleases you in a slightly different way, instead of six bottles of the same "Cab," which pleases you the same way every time?

Q: *What about buying wine "futures," which I have seen advertised?*

A: The presumed strategy behind buying "futures" is to lock in the lowest price on a particular wine by buying it before it is shipped to your wine shop and perhaps even before it has been bottled. Most often, futures offers apply to the best chateaus of Bordeaux. And that is where it makes the most sense. Traditionally, the wines of Bordeaux are first offered in a *première tranche*—"first cut"—in the spring after the vintage. Whoever buys it then will get the lowest price but must wait for as long as eighteen months until the wine is released. If the vintage is judged to be a success, later releases will be priced higher—perhaps much higher.

A bare few California wineries have begun to offer futures. But this market is in its uncertain infancy. Town Wines is one of the few retailers to offer a variant on futures which it calls "pre-arrivals." These are wines that have been purchased on one of the management's twice-yearly buying trips and are soon to arrive at the shop. They will cost about 15 percent more once they are on the retail shelves. Buying California pre-arrivals has two advantages over Bordeaux futures: 1) They usually arrive much sooner and 2) the wines have been tasted—in the case of Town, at least—by the shop's management before they were purchased. That doesn't mean you will also approve. But pre-tasting certainly narrows the chances that you will be disappointed.

Q: *You mentioned Town's California buying trips. Is that commonly done by wine shop personnel?*
A: It's not common. But it ought to be. The shop's proprietors, Stanley and Elliot Fishbein or wine manager Nick Zeiser visit California to find new wineries and renew acquaintances with old ones. During a two- or three-week stint they will visit at least fifty wineries, not all of them easy to reach. I was with them as a tag-along, for example, one April morning years ago when their rental car refused to make the last, extra-steep leg of a mountain road that led to the remote Santa Cruz

Mountain Vineyards. We hiked the rest of the way. Ken Burnap, proprietor of this tiny winery, more than repaid the effort by opening for us a bottle of his 1977 Pinot Noir, which remains the most magical California expression of this difficult grape I've tasted.

Out of the exhausting agenda of those trips (you don't always feel like tasting even good wine at eight o'clock in the morning) come the myriad "personal" wines that set one shop very much apart from another. Ambitious new wineries typically get so involved with making the best possible wine that they neglect the machinery of marketing it. They often have no distribution means beyond the borders of their state—or, for that matter—within them. The only way their wines will appear in a shop three thousand miles away is if the proprietor first comes knocking and then arranges his own transportation back east. Winemakers like Burnap, I noted, took heart at Fishbein's insistence on shipping only in refrigerated trucks.

Q: *Do you have any final thoughts on what makes a good wine shop?*

A: A good wine store is not a place where people dash in for their needs and dash out. It needs browsers the way a good bookstore does. It needs people to poke around and a staff that recognizes that need. I've had wonderful wines recommended to me by other browsers and have recommended some in return. It can be as great a service to warn, or be warned, against a wine. The quality of an establishment's clientele, incidentally, has always been taken into account by those much feared inspectors from *Guide Michelin* in arriving at their restaurant ratings along with more obvious factors like quality of food, service, and ambiance. No business with a highly personal imprint on it—and a fine wine shop is that as much as a fine restaurant —can flourish unless management and clientele are equally demanding of each other.

WINING
OUT

It ought to be to fun to choose a wine from a restaurant's wine list—but too often that isn't the case at all. It ought to be possible, as well, to get that wine at a reasonable price. Restaurants, after all, buy their wine wholesale. They do not have, as with food, either hefty preparation or spoilage costs to justify jacking up the price. But all too often the wine list at American restaurants is overpriced, even when the food is not. And yet the civilized pleasure of dining well in a public place, amid others, isn't the same unless wine is part of the occasion.

Ordering wine can, unfortunately, become an especially daunting prospect in a "fancy" restaurant (or one that is merely pretentious!). When you are handed that oversized, mock leather and guilded tome that is the wine list, decisions can suddenly become very hard to make with confidence—much harder than in a wine store. If the restaurant is French, you may find yourself staring at page upon page of names that mean nothing to you: Puligny-Montrachet, Les Pucelles; Chateau Malartic-Lagravière, Volnay Premier Cru, Clos de la Pousse d'Or; etc. Meanwhile, the inevitably suave and vaguely supercilious fellow in the tux hovers over the table, awaiting your command. Do you detect the outline of a smirk on his face? It's probably there. He knows that he might as well have handed you a list of irregular Latin verb forms.

It ought to be easier to choose a wine in restaurants where the new American cuisine and wines from our own soil reign. The preferred language, for one thing, is English. And the formality of European waiters has usually been banished in favor of a "just plain folks" style of service in which the staff may wear running shoes. But it is in just such a restaurant that the wine list can be trickiest of all.

What makes that list so tricky is that amid the rush of new wines from all over the land, we haven't had time yet to organize and categorize the fruit of the vine so well as have the French, with their centuries of winemaking behind them. The French way of winemaking is much more set than ours. Look, for example, at the wines of Bordeaux. Despite infinite subtle variations among the thousands of these wines containing a preponderance of Cabernet Sauvignon grapes, all are recognizably from the same family. This is not so, however, with American wines based on the identical grape. They range from light, stylish wines, in the Bordelaise mode, to "killer" wines of such enormous intensity that they would flatten a Frenchman. You may never know which is which, glossing a wine list, until it is too late.

In sum, a restaurant is a far trickier environment in which to make a correct wine selection than a wine shop is—let alone in your own home. There isn't a lot of time to poke around. And you must pick not only a good wine but one that will make sense with the food you will be served. You won't always make the ideal choice. But you will be satisfied more often if you think out certain moves in advance.

DEALING WITH THE WINE LIST

Q: *What should my first move be?*

A: Ask your waiter for the wine list even before you get the menu—especially when you are new to a restaurant. If you're planning to have a white wine, now is the time to have it brought to your table, to be sipped while discussing the menu, rather than when food arrives. Normally, you'd turn to the wine list only after you've ordered from the menu. That way you choose wine to accompany the food. But an early perusal of the list may turn up a wine to which you'd like to match the food you'll order, rather than the other way around. This could be a wine that's lived in your memory from a previous occasion. Or it might be a wine you've heard is excellent. Or it might simply be a wine that catches your fancy.

Finally, the wine list will often tell you more about a restaurant, in certain ways, than the menu. It isn't possible, frankly, for the management to care about food and not care about wine. Their harmony is essential to a fine meal. Each will elevate the pleasure of the other. So the level of attention to what is to be on your plate had better be reflected in the wine list.

Q: What makes a wine list good?

A: Selection and price. The selection needn't be huge to be good. New restaurants, in particular, may not have the funds to stock a large cellar. But small can be beautiful if the wines are chosen with care and imagination. There should be wines that will match every dish that the kitchen presents. If the menu is balanced, so should the wine list be. If the restaurant specializes in seafood, the list should be top-heavy in white wines. (The wine list of the famed Oyster Bar, in Manhattan's Grand Central Station, consists of dozens upon dozens of whites and no reds at all!). At a steakhouse, the list ought to be tilted toward reds, at least a few of them well aged.

The very best list, however, will lose its appeal if prices are not reasonable.

Q: How do you decide if prices on a wine list are reasonable?

A: You have several rules of thumb. Here is one that is very nearly (but not quite) absolute:

NO BOTTLE ON THE WINE LIST SHOULD COST MORE THAN DOUBLE ITS CURRENT PRICE AT RETAIL.

The economics behind this rule are simple enough. In most states, the wine you buy has been marked up by 50 percent. Thus, a $5 bottle at wholesale will retail at $7.50. If the restaurateur sells that bottle for $15, he is tripling his cost. If he hikes the price more than that, he is greedy—though a chorus of proprietors with overpriced wine lists will surely respond: "We have such high costs for rent, labor, and food that we have to make up for a low profit margin on the menu with a high margin on wine."

Don't accept that defense of the inflated markup. Most of us are willing to pay for value received. We expect that a superb meal won't come cheap. The use of top-quality ingredients, expertly prepared and handsomely presented, ensures that. But unless the wine you order is being served in Baccarat full-lead crystal replaceable at $50 per glass, the cost of wine service is minimal compared with the cost of food service. That's why I say that if wine prices are jacked up to more than triple the wholesale price, then the active element is, incontrovertably, greed.

Q: What if I don't know the retail cost of a wine?

A: Here's another rule of thumb: A range of bottles ought to be available at about the cost of the main course. If veal marengo is priced at $10.50, for example, then you should be able to select a wine for the same price. And I do mean select. There isn't any reason why there can't be at least a few wines, both red and white, at that price level. I'll go one step further and say that each and every American restaurant that is serious about offering wine value to its customers ought to have at least one red and one white wine for under ten dollars per bottle. Even an establishment as august as The Four Seasons on Park Avenue manages to tuck away a few wines in that class on its enormous list (like the co-owners, Tom Marghetai and Paul Kovi, these bargain wines were born in Hungary).

Q: Why dwell so much on price?

A: It's the first order of discussion for good reason. If the restaurant's wine prices are too far out of line, then you should respond by not buying any wine. You have no obligation to be gypped. Ask for lots of refills on icewater—which is good for you anyway. And don't hesitate to tell management exactly why you passed over the wine list. If the same message is gotten across from other diners who had heretofore acceded meekly to inflated prices, then a new and more reasonably priced wine list will soon be forthcoming.

Q: Now that we've dealt with pricing, how does one go about choosing wine that will complement the different dishes that have been ordered?

A: At home, this isn't a problem. Everyone shares in the one meal that's been prepared. Eating out, however, one diner might select striped bass on a purée of red pepper, while the person across the table has a yen for double lamb chops. For the fish, the wine list's best choice might be a spirited, not totally bone-dry Sauvignon Blanc. For the chops, there's a Cabernet Sauvignon that ought to be just right. Unfortunately, neither of these wines will "cross over" to the other dish. And you're only two diners. You don't each need a bottle of wine. It's a problem with several solutions.

Q: What about a bottle of rosé?

A: That's the traditional compromise when neither red nor white wine will serve both diners. A rosé is what its color implies—not quite red, not quite white. Too often, the wine lacks the better qualities of fine reds or whites. It's not that it's bad. It just has a case of the blahs. Those rosés that do have real personality usually have been made from the Granache grape. Three of the best are made by Robert Mondavi, McDowell Valley, and Washington's Chateau Ste. Michelle.

Q: *Why not avoid rosé altogether and order a half bottle each of red and white wine?*

A: By all means—if the management has been considerate enough to offer a choice of wines in halves. The only drawback here, in the case of two diners, is that you've now got the equivalent of a full bottle of wine. That's a total of eight glasses. If you're prepared to drink four glasses each, fine. If you aren't prepared, you probably will end up doing so anyway. One solution is to order a half bottle of white wine. Each of you then sips a glass as an apéritif. That will leave two glasses for the one who ordered the striped bass. Then the lamb chop eater can order a glass or a small carafe of the "house" red wine.

Q: *Should one hesitate to order the "house" wine?*

A: In theory, it should be possible to order a "house" wine with confidence. In fact, it often disappoints. The sad fact is too many restaurants with otherwise admirable standards can't seem to resist serving a "house" wine of pedestrian quality. Or overpricing one of decent quality. Or both.

This situation was brought home to me, shortly before this writing, at a lunch on the patio of an exceptional restaurant called Cafe in the Barn, located in Seekonk, Massachusetts. What the French call *cuisine soignée*—roughly translated as "pampered food"—is the rule here. In a very different category was the glass of "house red" I'd ordered. Here was a case where you could see disaster in the glass. In place of clarity and sparkle was a liquid that was dull and dark. Even the bright midday sunlight couldn't pierce it. The taste was as muddy as the look. My first reaction was to send it back with the waitress. Then I decided it would be a better learning experience if I brought the glass back to the bar myself to find out how this particular liquid had come to arrive at my table.

The bartender was a cheerful young woman who readily showed me the source of this wine—a gallon jug of inexpensive California Zinfandel from the fertile but hot San Joaquin Valley. California, we know, is justly honored for the high quality of its jug wines. This was the exception—a spoiled jug. But even if it had been of normal quality, this wine did not belong in such a restaurant. Sold by the glass, however, it was exceptionally profitable. Thirty generous glasses can be poured from a gallon jug. At a seemingly reasonable $1.50 per glass, that's $45 generated from a jug that wholesales for about $5. That's good from the bookkeeper's standpoint, but less so from that of the innocent drinker.

It would be comforting but inaccurate to say that the Cafe in the Barn was an exception to the would-be rule that a fine kitchen means a fine house wine. Too many negative experiences show it isn't so. (Other restaurants, in fact, charge as much as $3 for the same glass of plonk, bringing the proceeds of a jug up to $90!). But if the house wine remains under consideration, ask for its identity before ordering.

Q: *Is there any hope for the person who wants a decent single glass of wine?*

A: More than hope. A new type of machine, of which the best known is called Cruvinet, allows for the absolutely impeccable service of a single glass of wine from a bottle that may have been open for days. These machines put a layer of inert nitrogen gas into the neck of a freshly uncorked bottle. That keeps the air out, preserving the wine as well as if it has never been opened—perhaps better. When a glass of wine is ordered, it is drawn through a vacuum tube that has been inserted into the bottle.

The Cruvinet machine allowed for the birth of the new institution known as the wine bar. These casual spots are springing up all over America, having gotten their start in London and Paris. All have in common one or more big glowing brass and silvery Cruvinets with a variety of bottles attached. The largest, as of this writing, is at the Green Street Wine Bar in the Soho section of Manhattan, with 110 wines "on tap." You might pay as little as $1.50 for a glass of fresh young Chenin Blanc, or as much as $18 for a glass of forty-year-old Madeira. Light but often imaginative foods are increasingly available at such places —it's a wonderful venue in which to try out a selection of wines with your food that would otherwise be impracticable, to put it mildly. The day will come when Cruvinets won't be limited to wine bars. All serious restaurants will have them as well.

THE WINE SERVICE

Q: What do I do when the waiter presents the bottle we've selected for inspection?

A: Check to see that the vintage shown on the wine list is the vintage on the label. Often, the indicated vintage has been sold out, to have been replaced with another, as yet unlisted—and quite likely, not as good. The 1978 Bordeaux, for example, were uniformly superb. The 1977s were uniformly poor. Chances are, you'll order the 1978 and get the 1977, rather than the other way around. Don't accept a bottle that you know or suspect to be of a vintage inferior to the one that's listed.

With American wines, especially those from California, you needn't be so wary of switched vintages. While growing seasons do differ in character from year to year, they are never so cold as to leave the grapes just plain unripe, as happens to European wines. *What is critical in the case of domestic bottles is that you be sure that the wine is neither too young or too old.* The list might show a five-year-old Cabernet Sauvignon from a superior winery like Simi, for example. At that age, the wine has had a chance to "round out." If you are presented instead with a three-year-old Simi, you will have lost two critical years of that harmonizing process.

In the case of white wines, on the other hand, beware of bottles that are too old. Only Chardonnay and a very few sweet Rieslings benefit from a few years of bottle age. Chenin Blanc, Sauvignon Blanc, and nearly all other white wines are best when they are fresh. "Blush" wines, like white Zinfandel, fade most quickly of all. If you are offered a bottle more than two years old, don't accept it. The age question in the case of sparkling wines is moot, more often than not, since unvintaged blends are in the majority. The most noteworthy exception are those of Chateau Saint Jean—all vintage-dated. In any event, sparklers are always ready to drink when released (unlike the best still wines) and they neither gain nor lose much with a few years of bottle age—provided they have been properly stored.

Q: *What is this business of being handed the cork?*

A: The waiter's presentation to you of the freshly pulled cork is an honored part of wine ritual—and one that has long outlived its usefulness. In an earlier age, you would have immediately smelled the cork. And with good reason. Corks were frequent carriers of organisms that had infected the wine, giving it an off taste. The wine was then pronounced to be "corked" and sent back. In our time, however, corks arrive at the winery sterilized, which has eliminated cork "disease" in all but the rarest cases. I do admit to smelling an old cork for pleasure—especially if the bottle has come up from a damp cellar. It usually has a woodsy, mushroomy aroma that somehow sets a suitable mood for an old wine.

The other, equally outmoded reason that the cork has been traditionally handed over for inspection is so that the client can see that the brand on the cork corresponds to the label of the wine that is on the bottle before him. In earlier times, it seems, scurrilous restauranteurs were not above putting a famous label on a cheap bottle of wine and pricing it as if it were the real thing. But it was not so easy to replicate the branded cork. (Though rarely seen anymore, thin wire nets around bottles of wine with a good name were another way of ensuring that the wine in the bottle was as specified.)

Now that you know the background of the cork presentation ritual, you can in good conscience ignore it. Just put the cork aside and get on to the next —and more important—step....

Q: ... *The pouring of a splash of wine in my glass?*

A: Exactly. You must now approve or disapprove of the tendered bottle. This can be a bit of an uncomfortable moment. It's as if the chef were to come from the kitchen and hang over your first bite of the food he's devised. Don't make a big deal of this. If the glass is of a decent size, you can swirl the wine an instant or so to bring up the aroma. This is most easily and safely done by keeping the base of the glass on the table and giving it a very slight forward and backward motion. This will actually impart a circular motion to the wine in the glass.

Now take a quick, deep sniff. One is all you need. If the wine smells good, it will almost surely taste good. You needn't even sip the wine before giving your affirmative nod. If, on the other hand, the wine smells odd, bad, or doesn't smell at all, then by all means sip—but don't swallow. Swish the wine for a few seconds to determine what it tastes like. Bear in mind, though, that the first sip of any wine is often the least pleasant. The tannic edge of red wine will seem harsh in the absence of food. And white wine sometimes reveal a bit of sulfur dioxide—the same that you smell in lighting a match—which will quickly "blow off."

Q: *If I'm disappointed in the wine, what do I tell the waiter?*

A: Be clear, first, on the nature of that disappointment. Is it that the wine is faulty? Or is it that the wine is sound but not in the style you were expecting? Or are you just not quite sure? Ask the waiter for another splash of wine in your glass. This will alert him that you are troubled by the wine but aren't making a snap judgment. Pay attention to the color. If it's cloudy or opaque in the case of a red wine or slightly brown or deep golden in the case of a white, that's a sure sign that the wine is bad. Point out what you see to the waiter. He or she should whisk away the bottle before another word is said.

Q: *But what if the wine looks fine and the taste is "almost" okay—but not quite?*

A: Then don't hesitate at this moment to get an opinion from another person at your table. If you are both in agreement that the wine is faulty, tell the waiter forthrightly exactly what is displeasing you. To announce that it's a "bad bottle" won't suffice. Stick to the most vivid layperson's words you can summon up: "Vinegary," "rotten eggy," "like sherry instead of table wine," or just plain "sour." Trust your taste buds.

Q: *What if the waiter insists the bottle is good?*

A: Don't discuss the wine any further with the

waiter. Ask that the maître d' or manager be called to your table. If you have honestly and clearly set forth your reason for rejecting a wine, it will be exceedingly rare to meet resistance at management level. These people know well the difference between a genuinely dissatisfied diner and one who is merely trying to show off. Very serious wine lists, replete with old and prestigious items, occasionally bear the printed caveat that bottles of this type are sold at the client's risk. But unless you're planning on spending a few hundred dollars for, say, a thirty-year-old Chateau Haute-Brion, this "no-return" policy should never apply to you.

Q: Should I expect white wine to be served in an ice bucket?

A: We assume that white wines ought to be chilled. And they should be. But "chilled" isn't specific enough. Lighter, zippier wines, like Riesling, Chenin Blanc, and Sauvignon Blanc, are best when they are coldest. The same goes for sparkling wines. It's not enough that the bottle arrive in an ice bucket. It should have been pre-chilled so that you don't have to wait fifteen minutes for it to come down to the proper temperature of about 45 degrees. Sweet wines should also be chilled to the maximum, since as they warm up, their sweetness becomes more pronounced. It can become too much of a good thing.

The chilling of Chardonnay, unlike that of other wines, ought to be handled exceedingly gently. The range of complex flavors this grape can offer begins to be muffled as the wine's temperature dips into the low fifties. It's astonishing, by contrast, how flavor hidden by the cold will flower as the wine is allowed to "thaw." This lesson was impressed upon me years ago when I brought a bottle of old Chardonnay to the home of Harriet Lembeck, director of the Wine Program of the New York Wine & Food Society.

"Let's open it now," said this lover of old Chardonnays. She paid no heed to my warning that the wine was too warm. And it turned out that as we sipped that wine at just under room temperature, its every nuance came front and center. Ever since then, I've taken care to serve older Chardonnays with only a bit of chilling. Younger or lesser Chardonnays, in which subtlety is replaced by a more direct thrust of fruit, ought to be served a bit more chilled—but never so much as the lighter wines. A temperature in the upper fifties for the older wines and in the lower fifties for younger ones is about right. If the Chardonnay you've ordered arrives in an ice bucket, don't hesitate to have it removed directly to the table until it warms up a bit. You've paid for the full flavor of Chardonnay, and you may as well get it.

Q: *Should I be concerned with the temperature at which red wine is served?*

A: Red wine can be undermined by the wrong serving temperature as surely as white wine. It is most likely to come to the table too warm. Even if the dining room is air-conditioned, wine may be stored in a hot pantry. A Cabernet Sauvignon served in excess of 70 degrees is a wilted wine. Young, light reds, like Beaujolais or American Gamay, should be sipped at an even lower temperature than Cabernet. Sixty degrees is just about right. Feel the bottle when it arrives. If it's warmer than the dining room, ask if it can be put in an ice bucket for a few moments. The waiter may smile indulgently, as if you don't know what you're doing. Never mind.

Q: *Should a red wine be uncorked in advance of its drinking?*

A: It's common wisdom that certain "big" reds, like an intense Cabernet Sauvignon or Petit-Syrah, need air to smooth out their tannins and bring out their fullest flavor. The truth is that such a process may take longer than even your most leisurely sojourn in the restaurant. (The Italian red called Barolo is often opened the day before the meal!) The wines that may actually benefit most from airing, I've found, are Pinot Noirs, which seem light at first but amplify in flavor quite a bit after half an hour or so. Ideally, these wines should be decanted to give them that airing most efficiently. But few restaurants are prepared to decant your wine. The best you can do, in lieu of decanting, is to have the bottle opened at the beginning of your meal. Try it immediately. If it seems "closed up," have the wine poured a few minutes before the arrival of the main course. Breathing time in the glass is much more efficient than breathing time in bottle. And do let the bottle remain in sight even if a different wine is being served with a first course. Anticipation will build.

Q: *How often should a waiter refill glasses?*

A: Not so often or so zealously as some waiters do. It is particularly irritating when glasses are filled nearly to the rim. A normal-sized wine glass (six to twelve ounces) need be at most half-full. That leaves room for your nose as well as for the any bouquet the wine may have. It's also irksome when a waiter swoops in constantly to keep "topping out" the glasses. You can get the feeling that such a waiter is merely anxious to empty one bottle in order to sell another. If the wine-pouring is too fast, tell the waiter to stretch it out. Or simply put the flat of your hand above the glass if he is about to refill before you're ready.

Q: *Does it ever make sense to buy the oldest and most expensive bottle on the wine list?*

A: Only if these three conditions are met: 1) You discuss with sommelier or waiter the possibility that the wine may have gone "over the hill." Must you pay for the bottle if that's the case? Be satisfied on this point. 2) Fine, thin-lipped glassware is provided. 3) The waiter will decant the wine so as to leave behind the bottle sediment that has been built up over the years.

I haven't mentioned the cost factor of a rare old bottle, because anyone contemplating such a wine obviously isn't worried about the tab. But, paradoxically, the most expensive wines on the list are often the most reasonable in terms of markup. Raymond Sokolov once wrote in the *Wall Street Journal* of sampling a magnum (double bottle) of Chateau Haut-Brion 1948 at Windows on the World, atop the World Trade Center. At $165, the bottle cost about the same as at retail. The restaurant's wine director, Kevin

Zraly, had an answer to this. The restaurant makes its money on middle-priced wine, he told Sokolov, not on those at the extreme ends of the list.

Q: *Is there any reason to select American wines instead of imports when in a restaurant?*

A: Put pleasure before patriotism at the table and select the wine that offers the most in price and value. But do remember that American red wines— Cabernet Sauvignon especially—do tend to be more "giving" than their French counterparts at an early age. And it is young wines which most frequently appear on restaurant wine lists. It can take a decade or more for a stern Bordeaux to "come around." Five years is usually adequate for even the best American reds to show their best.

NOTES
FOR
SPECIAL
MEALS

THANKSGIVING

Nobody else but us North Americans celebrate Thanksgiving. Even the turkey is a natively American bird, unseen in Europe until its importation by six-teenth-century Spaniards. Propriety, patriotism, and a sense of history demand that on this day we serve the bird with wines of our own soil. Just which wines they should be is less clear.

Turkey is reported to be the stupidest of all com-mercially raised birds. It is surely the blandest in fla-vor. If a bird has been frozen too long and then cooked inattentively, the white meat could be mis-taken for cardboard that has been soaked in broth and wrung out. Even a fresh turkey that has been well seasoned and frequently basted during roasting will never be, except for its crispy skin, a powerhouse of assertive flavor. But it will always be a good partner to almost any fine wine, red or white. What the bird has been stuffed with will be the swing factor in choosing the particular wine.

The old standby stuffing, of fresh bread crumbs, chopped celery and onions, broth, and butter brings extra texture and flavor enrichment to the turkey without introducing any aggressive flavor of its own.

Adding oysters to that basic stuffing, New England—style, will bring yet another layer of intriguing flavor to the bird. In both cases, I'd look to a crisp, flavory white wine—a medium-weight Chardonnay like those from Landmark or Grand Cru, or a Chenin Blanc in the off-dry style of Pedroncelli or Parducci. That touch of sweetness has one decided advantage over the austere Chardonnay: it won't do combat with either the cranberry sauce or candied sweet potatoes that traditionally share the Thanksgiving plate.

The wine picture shifts when the stuffing contains sausage meat and, typically, apples or other fruit as well. Now a more assertive wine is in order. My preference would still be a white wine—but just barely. An aromatic, spicy, Gewürztraminer would provide that extra thrust of personality. Again, it will best harmonize with the rest of the plate if it is off-dry. Clos du Val and Hacienda make a wonderfully vigorous "Gewürz" in this style.

The shift to red wine comes, for me, with the addition to the stuffing of chestnuts, wild rice, and dried mushrooms that have perhaps been soaked in port or Madeira. If the stuffing isn't too assertively spicy or herby, I'd choose a Pinot Noir in the medium price range (under ten dollars) from one of the Oregon specialists in that grape or perhaps the BV "Carneros" bottling. If a luxury bottling is in order, Chalone and Acacia aren't likely to disappoint. I'd shift wines again, however, if the stuffing carries the thrusting flavor of sage or rosemary. This time it would be to Zinfandel. A rich but not overly alcoholic rendition would be in order, like those of Fetzer, De Loach, and McDowell Valley. Though Zinfandel is rarely planted outside of California, a version is offered by Chicama, of Martha's Vineyard, Massachusetts, a two-hour boat ride from where Pilgrims and Indians sat down together to the first Thanksgiving meal. Unfortunately, this wine's flavor is no match for its pedigree.

The long and festive Thanksgiving meal won't draw to its traditional close until the pies—including mincemeat—are set out. This is the moment to offer one and all a glass of American port, late-harvest Zinfandel, or Quady's Elysium or Essencia (see page 117). These are wines for which the season must be right as well as the food. And this final Thursday of November, when autumn crispness and color have finally given way to the unforgiving chill of oncoming winter, is the time to strike back with these deep and warming wines.

THE CHRISTMAS DINNER

The order of the Christmas dinner isn't so restrictive as that of Thanksgiving. Dinner might be built, English-style, around a standing rib roast with Yorkshire pudding, in which case a Pinot Noir, Merlot, or Petite-Syrah will bring the proper plump richness. If game is available, the same choices hold, whether it is venison or duck on the platter. Should a ham be baking in the oven, the choice of wines is touchier. As Barbara Ensrud points out in her book *Food and Wine*, she and her husband had assumed in their youth that a dry red wine was a "must" with ham if one was to be a sophisticated person. As she and we have since learned (once we shed our preconceptions), a far more pleasing match for ham would be an off-dry "blush" Zinfandel. Hard apple cider is, truthfully, an even better choice.

The fruitcakes and puddings of the season take well to an American port or other fortified wine. And, it goes almost without saying, the two beverages that must be at the ready on Christmas day are eggnog and sparkling wine. Once, it would have been a risk to offer any sparkler other than genuine French Champagne. Now our American versions are numerous and of excellent quality.

PASSOVER

The range of American kosher wines could have been divided, not too many years ago, into sweet, sweeter, and sweetest. I loved them all—especially the syrupy blackberry wine ("specially sweetened" was the label term) over which the holiday blessings were pronounced. I love them still. But there comes a time, during the Passover meal, when something closer to the norms of table wine is wished for. That wish has been magnificently fulfilled, very recently, by the appearance of wines under the Hagafen (Hebrew for "the vine") label. They are kosher for Passover. Even if they weren't, they would still be superb.

Hagafen's 1984 Riesling is as appealing and as stylishly fine as any I've come across from California. The full range of red, white, and sparkling wines is offered by this winery. Most of the grapes come from

Winery Lake vineyards, in Carneros, which, except for Douglas Meader's Ventana Vineyards, has no rival as a supplier of superior, very expensive grapes to wineries that don't care to compromise. The wines are expensive ($9 for the Riesling, $13.50 for the Chardonnay, $12 for the Cabernet Sauvignon). Another new maker of superior kosher wines from California is Weinstock Cellars.

It's interesting to note that there is no rigorously detailed body of biblical or rabbinical law relating to the koshering of wine. The chief requirement seems to be that those who make it be observant Jews—observant enough, at least, not to eat a ham sandwich with one hand while operating the bottling line with the other.

WINE WITH CHINESE FOOD

In the wine world an eternal search goes on for the right wine, even the perfect wine, to act in harmony with the magnificent cuisine of faraway China. The problem with matching Oriental food to Occidental wine is that neither evolved with the other in mind. That doesn't mean successful matches can't be made. But they are few. Never, in my experience, have they been inspired. I'd go so far as to say that almost every dish in the brilliant and varied arsenal of Chinese dishes will almost always shoot down every fine *vinifera* wine that is put forward to match it. And for good reason. These wines, which in substance and style come to us from the French, exist to be ennobled by hollandaise sauces, cream sauces, Mornay and other cheese sauces, and beurre blanc. But neither butter nor egg yolks nor cream nor cheese has a place in the traditional Chinese kitchen. Fundamental to the glory of that kitchen, on the other hand, is the use—often unrestrained—of fresh ginger and fermented black bean, of garlic and soy sauce, of star anise and roasted sesame oil. With the exception of garlic, none of these assertive flavorings has a home in the traditional French kitchen. And if they are used, it's done very timidly indeed.

It's this chasm between basic seasonings that is the problem. When a steamed or poached flounder comes out of a French kitchen, for example, it will most likely be bathed in a beurre blanc or white sauce made from reduced fish stock and cream. The dish will go marvelously with any of a number of delicate white wines, like Riesling and Chenin Blanc. But those wines turn problematic when accompanying that flounder as prepared by a Cantonese chef who has accented the flatfish's delicate flesh by first crosshatching the skin and inserting within slivers of ginger and black beans and then steaming it. You can certainly drink those light, fruity whites with the flounder. But the pungency of ginger and black bean won't allow for the same subtle harmony between fish and wine.

The problem of food and wine matches is no less with red meats. The French chef, for example, typically seasons leg of lamb with garlic, rosemary, and perhaps a bit of mustard before roasting. No more perfect dish was ever created for red Bordeaux. A chef from Szechwan, on the other hand, would cut slivers of lamb off the bone and stir-fry it with a blast of hot peppers. The poise of a mature red Bordeaux would be obliterated by the heat. Only the tannins would stand firm. With your gums already singed by those slender but nearly lethal green and red peppers, tannin is exactly what you *don't* need.

This problem of which wine to drink with Chinese food, I'm afraid, goes quite beyond the question of any specific case. It has to do with a whole different style, rhythm, and weight of the Chinese meal. What else can you say about a formal dinner that ends, traditionally, with clear soup? If in place of that soup the host were to have said, "Bring on the cheese platter with the Nuits-Saint-Georges" the Chinese guests would have been mystified.

My advice is to give up trying to find the perfect wines to match Chinese food. As French wines evolved regionally to make sweet harmony with French foods, so Chinese wines would have to have evolved with Chinese food. But they didn't. Throwing the wines we love into that void is never going to make up for an evolution that didn't happen. That doesn't mean you can't sip a Gewürztraminer or Sauvignon Blanc with moderately spicy food or a Chenin Blanc with that steamed flounder or a Zinfandel with stir-fried Szechwan. But don't expect much more than coexistence. The most serviceable single wine may actually be a cheap, slightly sweet sparkler. André is ideal. Best of all, usually, is beer, icewater, or tea.

WINE FOR JAPANESE FOOD

The most popular Japanese dishes get along more easily with wine than those of China. At a sushi bar, you'll find any of a number of crisp, delicate white wines that will accompany most raw fish—though tuna or salmon, with their richer flesh, can take on a Chardonnay. A wine with a bit of sweetness, like an off-dry Chenin Blanc or Riesling, will go best with the batter-fried seafood and vegetables called tempura. Terriyaki beef, with soy and ginger, marinaded before being seared, delivers aggressive flavor. Even so, the prevailing style of the Japanese table is light, so I would be loath to accompany this dish with too weighty a wine. My choice would be a young Pinot Noir. Even when individual wine and food matches are made, however, their orchestration is not done along our own lines. Too much may be on the table at once to make sense out of wine service. Once again, you ought to have no compunction in forsaking wine for beer.

WINE FOR INDIAN FOOD

The most complex, intricately spiced, and to us perhaps the most alien of cuisines is that of India—shifting as it does from meat to vegetarian, from fiery vindaloos to the gentlest yogurt-smoothed fish dishes. Once again, however, there is no tradition of drinking wine with the meal. Interestingly, however, a group of top French chefs were officially invited to India early in 1985 in the hope that they would be inspired by their Indian counterparts to bridge two great culinary traditions. And so, according to food and wine writer David Rosengarten, at least a few of them were.

Later that year, Rosengarten reported in his *Wine Spectator* column that in Paris he had encountered a number of brilliantly successful dishes of Indian inspiration. Among them was tandoori rabbit accompanied by saffron rice, tomato chutney, spiced zucchini, and artichokes. To wash down this creation, Rosengarten expected the sommelier to propose some "blackened tannic monster" that wouldn't shrink back from such an array of exotic tastes and spicings. What came instead was an inexpensive and unsung young red Bordeaux—a wine never capable of sheer power. While Rosengarten doesn't rave about this wine and food combination, neither does he turn thumbs down.

At the restaurant Le Petit Pre, he exulted over "oysters with chervil and Madras curry, tiny rice-stuffed squid in a saffron sauce, artichoke hearts with coriander.... Sauces tasting of ginger and cardomon! Plates everywhere flashing tones of orange, yellow and red." The chef, Christian Verges, had firm thoughts on what wines ought to be served with Indian-influenced food. His strategy was not to attempt to match spice to spice but to serve simple, direct whites like Sauvignon Blanc and equally direct, spirited reds like young Bordeaux and, especially, the Loire reds Saumur-Champigny, Chinon, and Sancerre Rouge.

Most of California is a bit too sunny and warm to

consistently produce dashingly fresh and light-bodied wines in the French style that Verges prescribes. Actually, the East Coast is more adept at producing this kind of wine—a Seyval-Blanc from Pennsylvania's Allegro Vineyards, for example, or a Merlot from Long Island's Lenz Vineyards. My own wine choice for Indian food would be the same as for Chinese—a "blush" Zinfandel or a cheap sparkling wine.

WINES FOR A FOURTH OF JULY PICNIC AND OTHER EXPEDITIONS

The idea of a relaxed picnic usually outshines the reality. You hope for lovely weather, and you may indeed get it. But who really takes into account the flies, the bees, the spiders, the ants—a kingdom of all that crawls, united by an aggressive interest, in your carefully prepared food or, worse yet, onto the flesh. If the outing is at the beach, then sand is sure to get into the chicken salad, into the stuffed mushroom caps.... Is it really possible that nobody thought to bring a sharp knife to cut the homemade zucchini bread? And—oops!—how, exactly, did the vinaigrette seep out of its supposedly sealed container?

Later, we'll remember that succession of little catastrophes with amused affection and plot to do it all again. With wine, of course. The rule for picnics is simple: Abandon any refined tastes you may have developed. Keep the wine young, vivid, forthright, inexpensive, and, if possible, cool. Outdoors is where the generic wines like "burgundy" and "chablis" come into their element. It's the wrong environment for the most nuanced Cabernet Sauvignon and most Chardonnays. They just don't have the recreational spirit. Forcing these refined wines on picnic food is a bit like insisting that Marcel Proust participate in a rough game of mud tag.

For the cold cuts, patés, fried chicken, and other foods you'll bring to the picnic already cooked, it doesn't matter what you drink. If you are going to the trouble of grilling meats on the spot, however, you might as well also go to the trouble of bringing a wine forceful enough to stand up to the flavor of charcoal-seared burgers, steak, or chicken. The wine made for this purpose is Petite-Syrah—a dark, delicious, but rather one-dimensional red that will easily pierce the most darkly seared meats. Guenoc, Inglenook, McDowell Valley, and Concannon all make splendid versions of this wine at a moderate price.

If you're an Easterner contemplating a clam bake or a crab or shrimp boil, it was only a few years ago when your wine had to come from far away. Today there are established and incipient wineries up and down the New England and mid-Atlantic coast. Nearly all of them make better whites than reds. Here you'll find not only the *vinifera* wines, like Chardonnay and Riesling (a wine that turns out particularly well here), but the "crosses," or hybrids of Franco-American grapes like Vidal and Seyval-Blanc. Don't expect the full weight of California flavor or the racy finesse of the best French examples. But these wines are good and getting better. And, for once, what you are always told to ask for in the French countryside

—the *vin de la region*—will be your own.

I haven't made the crucial distinction above between family-style picnics, in which children will drop their food in dirt or sand when not disappearing, and the presumably more romantic picnics for two adults—perhaps taking place in a glen where nobody can see picnicking or any other activities. In this case, I would relent and say that you can bring along a more "sophisticated" bottle or two: A Chateau Montelena Zinfandel, perhaps, or a Chateau Saint Jean Fumé Blanc, and maybe even a half bottle of a sweet but spirited late-harvest Riesling or Gewürztraminer. But do it only if you also have invested in a handsome English wicker picnic kit that includes real plates, silverware, and wine glasses that actually are glass. It's less romantic but essential to tote along, in addition, a cooler. A final caveat: Sparkling wine is not meant for picnics unless you can be sure it will stay very cold. Lukewarm, it will be no treat. Even then, there's the peril of opening a bottle after a long and bumpy ride. You can lose an entire glass in the form of a geyser of froth.

AIRPLANE WINE

I can't be the only person of a certain age who remembers when the sight of a stewardess (now flight attendant) pushing the meal cart down the aisle of a commercial airliner (they weren't all jetliners then) was a positive event. It's no longer possible to know if the seeming excellence of those meals was a myth to be chalked up to their novelty and my innocence of long ago. What's certain is that today's meals aboard commercial flights are likely to be, in order of frequency, mediocre, downright poor, and—oh so occasionally—quite good.

It's not entirely fair, of course, to snipe too mercilessly at airline meals. Food that must be prepared in a commissary and then sent up into the sky to await reheating hundreds of thousands of miles away can't be held to a restaurant standard. What is inexcusable, however, is the service aloft of undistinguished wines of the blandest sort. There isn't a small winery in America that wouldn't be delighted, if only it were asked, to bottle up a wine of character and even of distinction for airline service. And yet the same commercial-grade European and American wines appear in their little screw-top bottles on most flights.

Purveyors of these wines would perhaps argue in their defense that the vast majority of passengers wouldn't know the difference between a wine with some personality and the normal, which is so bland. But that's no excuse. All of us who admire fine wine started out ignorant. We would have stayed that way if someone hadn't put a wine of real interest in front of us. Why not on an airplane?

My suggestion is that if you want to be sure to enjoy a good meal aboard a long flight, then bring it yourself—including the wine. A portion of roasted chicken or duck, sliced cold steak that has marinated in a mild mustard or ginger sauce, a really good chicken salad sandwich, or even a cold hamburger is preferable to the best that the flight attendant will offer you. Granted, there's not always the time to arrange for a take-aboard meal. But you can markedly upgrade the quality of the airline's meal by consuming it with your own choice of wine, specially brought along. It's called the power of association. Save and wash out one of those single-portion screw-top bottles. As close to flight time as possible, fill it with the last quarter of a wine that has given you pleasure. Ideally, it ought to be red wine, which won't need chilling. Nobody will even notice when you slip it out of your hand luggage. Don't neglect to take along a wine glass that is not too delicate, large, or expensive. Just be sure it is glass, rather than plastic.

Bringing your own wine aboard will admittedly take a bit of advance planning. But you will have dramatically upgraded the aesthetics of that meal on a tray. And remember to wash out that little bottle for the next time.

APPENDICES

APPENDIX I

A SAMPLING OF WINE AND FOOD MENUS

The menus below are composed of dishes that lean to the basic and that have an affinity for wine—more often than not, to the wine of a particular grape. I've selected specific wines with an eye toward those labels that are in reasonably broad distribution. (Refer to the chart in Appendix III for the ideal age for each wine.) You may choose, for each main course selection in this first group of menus, a wine in a range of three prices. You won't be shortchanging your dining partners by selecting the most modestly priced. As necessary, I've noted where a particular recipe can be found. Regretfully, I've omitted soups from these menus. Even at their wondrous best, they ask for a chunk of fresh, firm bread rather than a sip of wine. Finally, while dessert and wine matches are included, I adhere to the earlier opinion that most such pairings represent an overload on the palate—even when the flavors harmonize. You may decide otherwise.

A WINTER DINNER

Spaghetti with slow-cooked sliced onions
CHENIN BLANC
(in the off-dry style of Clos du Bois, Simi, or Pedroncelli)

~~~

Roast whole chicken cooked with carrots and green
beans

CABERNET SAUVIGNON
Beaulieu "Beautour" (lower-priced)
Beaulieu "Rutherford" (medium-priced)
Beaulieu "George de la Tour Private Reserve" (luxury)

~~~

Green Salad

~~~

Dried fruit tart

DESSERT WINE
(Ridge Zinfandel "Essence" or Quady "Essencia")

NOTE: This meal admittedly leans toward mild flavors. A
zestier first course—gazpacho or warm spicy sausage,
for example—would have offered greater contrast to the
chicken. But that wouldn't have done much for the
wines. Make no mistake about it: This meal will be
transformed by the selection of wines. They will provide
the enlivening edge of acid, alcohol, and flavor without
which the march of courses would be delicious but
rather too sedate.

The magnificently simple yet savory spaghetti with
slow-cooked sliced onions comes from Marcella Hazan's
More Clasic Italian Cooking. In my own kitchen, the
chicken—it's usually the meaty Perdue Oven Stuffer—
is cooked in a Romertorf clay pot, which is first soaked
in water. That water turns to steam within the pot during cooking, making for a moist bird, which somehow
also manages to turn golden brown without basting. The
vegetables also do beautifully in the pot, picking up flavorful juices from the chicken as they cook.

This is a meal, finally, for which the food cost will be
quite modest. Remind yourself of that when you are
buying the wine.

A SUMMER (WHITE WINE ONLY) DINNER

Leek and mushroom pie

SAUVIGNON BLANC (FUMÉ BLANC)
(Inglenook; Chateau Ste. Michelle, Washington; Sterling)

~~~

Grilled salmon basted with garlic, rosemary, and lemon butter; corn on the cob and creamed spinach

CHARDONNAY
Glenn Ellen Proprietor's Reserve (Low-priced)
Kendall Jackson Proprietor's Reserve (Medium-priced)
Sonoma Cutrer, "Les Pierres" Vineyard (Luxury)

~~~

Wedges of blue cheese and ripe pears

SWEET RIESLING
(Chateau Saint Jean Selected Late Harvest; Joseph Phelps Selected Late Harvest)

NOTE: When warm weather comes, the taste for red wine goes. Hence, the all-white-wine dinner. The leek and mushroom tart reaches its apex in Paula Wolfert's recipe in *The Cooking of South-West France*. Don't hesitate to substitute swordfish for salmon, according to availability. But bear in mind that it tends to dry out more quickly on the grill than the oilier salmon. You might also substitute a sweet Gewürztraminer for the sweet Riesling. Chateau Saint Jean makes a ravishing dessert-style "Gewürz."

A HOLIDAY DINNER

Oysters Rockefeller

SPARKLING WINE
(Korbel Brut; Domaine Chandon, Blanc de Noir; Piper
Sonoma Brut)

~~~

Standing rib roast
Yorkshire pudding, sautéed mushrooms, steamed
zucchini

PINOT NOIR
(Sokol Blosser or Eyrie, Oregon; Acacia, Calera or
Chalone)

~~~

Tomato salad

~~~

Vanilla ice cream, raspberry sauce

~~~

A bowl of walnuts and a plate of figs

CALIFORNIA PORT
(Ficklin, Quady, J. W. Morris)

NOTE: In an echo of Victorian tradition, it's nice to drift
to plump chairs in the living room or den for the pouring
of the port. The big difference between then and now, of
course, is that this pleasant finale to the meal is not limited to men.

A DO-AHEAD DINNER

Fish quenelles with white wine sauce

RIESLING
(Joseph Phelps, Early Harvest; Ste. Chapelle, Idaho;
Glenora, New York)

~~~

Lamb stew

MERLOT
Louis Martini (Low-Priced)
Gundlach-Bundschu, Rhinefarm (Medium-Priced)
Duckhorn (Luxury)

~~~

Green salad
A selection of cheeses

ZINFANDEL
(Fetzer; Ridge "Geyserville" or "York Creek"; Chateau
Montelena)

~~~

Rice pudding

ALMOND-FLAVORED SPARKLING WINE
(Franzia)

NOTE: Properly covered or wrapped, all of the above
dishes can be made the day before. A full discussion of
quenelles, as well as the recipe for the above dish, can
be found in *Mastering the Art of French Cooking, Volume One*.

The almond-touched sparkler that ends the meal
seems to have an affinity for rice pudding. The Franzia
is quite sweet, so you may prefer to blend your own at
the table. A tablespoon of Italian "amaretto" per glass is
just right. Use an inexpensive sparkler like Gallo's
André for this drink. The subtleties of a more expensive
wine would be mostly lost to by the almond flavoring.

TWO VEGETARIAN DINNERS

One needn't contemplate the matching of wines to a meatless menu with dismay. Butter, cream, cheese, mushrooms and grains all make classical harmonies with fine wine. Here are two sample menus.

MENU I

Batter-fried zucchini sticks

SAUVIGNON BLANC
(Gallo, Concannon, De Loach)
or

SEYVAL BLANC
(Easterners—pick a brand from your own or a neighboring state)

~~~

Buckwheat crepes filled with mushroom duxelles

PINOT NOIR
(Carneros Creek, Chateau Bouchaine, Sanford)

~~~

Mixed green salad

~~~

Crème Brûlée

SPARKLING WINE (off-dry)
(Almaden Golden; Schamsberg Cremant; Widmers Niagara, New York)

~~~

MENU II

Polenta with sauce of tomato, eggplant and sage

ZINFANDEL
(Pedroncelli, Sebastiani, Ridge)

~~~

Roquefort or Gorgonzola Cheese Soufflé
CHARDONNAY
(Landmark; Chateau Saint Jean; Wagner, New York)

~~~

Baked apple (winter), stewed rhubarb (spring), or fresh
berry compote (summer)

~~~

MORE SAMPLE MENUS

I've suggested a pair of wines for each of the menus below. In the usual case where a white and a red are contrasted, I haven't automatically followed the convention that white comes first. (You will only be able to evaluate that convention by occasionally violating it.) The choice of wine brands is left up to you in consultation with the staff of your wine shop. Don't hestitate to opt for the unknown. Your chances of being pleasantly surprised are, in this heyday of American wines, greater than your chances of being disappointed.

Baby squash sautéed with onion, wine, and lemon
PINOT BLANC

~~~

Chicken breasts with leeks and paprika
CABERNET SAUVIGNON

~~~

Watercress and Bibb lettuce salad

~~~

Orange sherbet and vanilla ice cream
Current cookies

Gnocchi with cream sauce

SPARKLING WINE

~~~

Veal chops with sage and white wine
Lacy potato pancakes
Batter-fried yellow squash slices

PINOT NOIR

~~~

Pears and Tallegio cheese

Peas with sausage, scrambled eggs, and fresh coriander

GEWÜRZTRAMINER (dry)

~~~

Portuguese steak (pan-fried in olive oil with garlic, red
wine, and prosciutto)
Fried potatoes
Baked tomatoes with parsley and basil

ZINFANDEL

~~~

Lime flan

Ravioli filled with goat cheese
PINOT BLANC

~~~

Veal Paillard
Braised celery and onion
Pureed carrots
CABERNET SAUVIGNON

~~~

Aruguola salad

~~~

Glazed brandied bread pudding

Moules Marniere (Mussels steamed in white wine)
SAUVIGNON BLANC

~~~

Loin of pork with prunes and cream
Home fried potatoes
Braised peas and lettuce
GAMAY

~~~

Deep dish blackberry cobbler

Philo dough stuffed with leeks and mushrooms
CHENIN BLANC

~~~

Baked fresh ham with apricot sauce
Slow-cooked carrots with parmesan cheese

Puree of string beans and potatoes
GRANACHE ROSÉ

~~~

Vanilla ice cream with dark chocolate sauce

Warm salad of sliced duck sausage, sliced boiled potatoes and watercress
MERLOT

~~~

Grilled flounder with white wine and grapes
Red cabbage and chestnuts
Rutabaga casserole
GERÜRZTRAMINER

~~~

Poached apples with almond topping

Egg and spinach soup

~~~

Scallops sautéed with slivers of country ham
Buttered peas
Coleslaw
REISLING or EMERALD RIESLING

~~~

A platter of assorted mild cheeses
CABERNET SAUVIGNON

Spaghetti with pesto sauce
SAUVIGNON BLANC or SEYVAL-BLANC

~~~

Roast duck
Whipped turnips and potatoes
Braised Swiss chard
PETITE-SYRAH

~~~

Tomato and Bermuda onion salad

~~~

Sour cherry pie

White bean and tuna salad
WHITE ZINFANDEL

~~~

Chicken breasts with a tarragon cream sauce
Wild rice sautéed with shitake mushrooms
Buttered green beans
PINOT NOIR

~~~

Green salad

~~~

Walnut cake

Maryland-style crab cakes
CHENIN BLANC or MUSCAT CANELLI

~~~

Boiled lobster
Buttered corn and sautéed spinach

CHARDONNAY

~~~

Tomato and cucumber salad

~~~

Strawberry shortcake

APPENDIX II

KEEPING A WINE LOG

You'll do yourself at least two favors by keeping a log of the wines you drink. The act of "thumbnailing" a wine in a few dozen words will, for one thing, force you to think with precision about its character. Talking through it just isn't the same. And once you've begun to accumulate entries, you're likely to find yourself getting little hits of pleasurable recognition as you reread them—much as you would from flipping through an old family photo album. It's not only the wine you'll remember, but the good times.

As for the format: Color, smell, and taste are the starting point for your evaluation. But don't be hemmed in by an imagined obligation to report specifically on that sensory triad. If the color of the wine is unremarkable, for example, then pass comment by. If, on the other hand, some odd but clarifying allusion pops into your head as you try to nail down the character of the wine, by all means note it.

Often a wine can best be put into perspective by comparing it with others of its kind (How does this Napa "Cab" stack up to last Saturday evening's version from the Santa Cruz Mountains?) If you are returning to a wine sampled previously, compare it with its earlier self. Chances are it won't be the same. Don't fret if you can't think of anything at all to say about a particular wine. Sometimes it happens—and it almost certainly means that the wine isn't distinctive enough to merit your written comment.

Excerpted below are a baker's dozen of entries from my own wine log, originally typed but now stored on a home computer disc. Saving wine labels, incidentally, is a bit of a bother, but it does provide a pleasing visual dimension to your notes. Unfortunately, the labels you most want are invariably the ones that least want to come off the bottle. If that's the case, just keep on soaking in warm water. Eventually the glue will loosen. A final suggestion: Take your notes on the spot, wherever you are, and transcribe them, if necessary, when you get home. In wine tasting, an immediate response is the best response.

DAVID BRUCE GEWÜRZTRAMINER (Edna Valley, San Luis Obispo County) 1978: This maker's wines are always a surprise in one way or another—beginning, in this case, with the color. It is an absolutely startling hue of pale salmon, or perhaps the color of an autumn oak leaf as it begins to turn to a more flamboyant shade of orange. The taste of the wine isn't out of line with that color: an enormously unsubtle, overly ripened taste which seems sweet at first, but then finishes dry—just as a good Alsatian "Gewürz" should. The French, who originated this type of wine, would despise an example with this much blunt force. I'm not French, and so I don't despise it. But I wouldn't want to drink this tiring, ungainly "Gewürz" again. The other bottle that I own will be used for cooking.

GALLO GEWÜRZTRAMINER (California) 1983: This wine shows both the virtues and limitations of wines in the Gallo empire. The virtue lies in its impeccable, "squeaky-clean" vinification. The acid and fruit are tuned just right. The limitation is self-imposed: a lack of varietal intensity and of distinctive personality. This is a wine whose first priority is to be on good behavior. It's like a pretty face lacking animation. Somewhere between the rather crazed David Bruce "Gewürz" above and this too tame Gallo example lies a style of wine that is more satisfying.

NAVARRO VINEYARDS GEWÜRZTRAMINER (Anderson Valley, Mendocino County) 1979: What makes this wine exceptionally pleasing is a precise marrying of grape character, snappy acid, and length of flavor. It is a harmonious wine. Just enough "Gewürz spiciness so you know it's not Riesling nor any other white grape. Just lean enough to pay homage to its Alsatian forebears. But giving enough to be pure California. A very nice job.

GREEN & RED ZINFANDEL (Chiles Canyon, Napa) 1977: At age six years, this wine still bites my gums with young tannins. But there's loads of deep, intense flavor here, too. At moments the wine seems to have a sweetness to it which is welcome against those tannins. Still, it's a wine that verges on the edge of being too fierce. But it does appear kinder when served with a ragu of beef.

FALL CREEK EMERALD RIESLING (Llano County, Texas) 1983: A first Texas wine for me, and there's nothing due but praise. The emerald Riesling best known to me is Paul Masson's—a more overtly spritzy, sweeter wine. This one is all delicacy, with melony, lemony flavors dancing lightly. While I'd never call it a watery wine, though, it seems almost a bit too delicate. But the subtlety carries it. At 11.4 percent, the alcohol is right where it should be.

CHATEAU CHEVALIER MERLOT (Napa) 1978: I have lost my earlier note on this wine. But I have no trouble remembering that when I first met this wine at the winery five years ago, the color alone—an exceptionally dark purple verging on black—left no doubt that the wine would be a powerhouse. And so it was. I'd rarely come across such concentrated richness. With time, it seemed, it would mellow to magnificence. I bought six bottles on that premise. But it hasn't panned out. Sipped with a beef stew on a winter's evening in 1986, this Cabernet hadn't mellowed a bit. In fact, it seemed to have taken on a few harder edges, while that lush Merlot had diminished. Rather than mellowing as the years go by, I'm wondering if this wine won't dry out and shatter. There's also a slight but definite spritziness in this wine which seems to indicate some fault in the winemaking.

GLENORA CHARDONNAY (Dundee-on-Seneca, New York) 1979: At five years of age, this wine was buttery, intense, full and "big league" by any standard. The label claimed it showed "great promise" for bottle development. Absolutely right. I wouldn't have wanted to drink this wine earlier. It was bought at half price in an otherwise savvy Manhattan shop as a "bin end." It should have been on a shelf of honor.

MARTIN RAY CHARDONNAY (Winery Lake, Carneros Region of Napa) 1979: Martin Ray wines have a reputation for roving out of the mainstream, as this one certainly does. It's an intense Chardonnay with nice body—clearly a wine with presence. But what stands out is an assertive nutmeg taste which is out of phase with normal Chardonnay character. And, except for a first reaction of intrigue, I can't say that it is welcome. Not my favorite wine. (Later note: Met the grower, Mr. di Rosa, at a Napa tasting in New York. Asked him about that odd nutmeg taste. He said that Martin Ray's old cooperage is what imparts that flavor, not the grape itself.)

BERINGER CABERNET SAUVIGNON (State Lane Vineyard, Napa) 1979: Tasted in 1983: Of California's diverse styles of "Cab," this is the classic to come back to with gratitude: brilliant, not too dense purple hue, a lovely, vinous nose, and a refined taste of black currants melded into smooth texture. And how that flavor does linger! I bought this wine because I'd read that it won a "best of show" at a major wine competition. No disagreement here.

Retasted in 1985: The color has begun to turn a

more mature garnet. The nose has deepened and so has the flavor. It's gone from that lively black currant to a deeper, richer plum that lingers long in the mouth. The texture is silken. This is a wine both calm and filled with life. I'm certain that with age it will only take on more graces.

LA CREMA VINERA PINOT NOIR (Sonoma), Lot A-0/1: Everyone who has been seduced by a bottle of Burgundian Pinot Noir doing its ineffable "thing" hopes to duplicate the experience on turf removed from the Côte d'Or. Magic, however, isn't easily or often duplicated. This wine does manage to be a ringer for a good Burgundy. It has that fatness and expansive flavor without being in the least heavy. Even the color is pale like true Burgundy. The hitch is that the magic isn't there. Absent are those gentle silky fingers that caress and that light touch backed up by reserves of power only hinted at. To be fair to this well-made wine, however, I must say that French Burgundies nowadays don't achieve exalted status either. Most don't even taste this good.

GROTH SAUVIGNON BLANC (Napa) 1982: The wine struck me as having a finer texture and more polish than most wines made from this forceful grape, whose scent and flavor are typically compared to freshly mown grass. It also seemed to have a touch of oak aging that balanced the fruit flavors perfectly. But the food and wine writer Barbara Kafka, who was at the same table, had a totally different opinion. In fact, she practically gagged on the wine, insisting that it had made from grapes that were unripe.

One month later: This wine turned up on the wine list of a Manhattan restaurant called Pesca and I jumped at the chance to try it again. Perhaps it was the power of suggestion, but it did now seem to me that perhaps, behind that still fine texture of the wine, there was a bit of sourness. But I'd be happy to drink the wine again. And I still find it to be a cut above most other Sauvignon Blancs in texture and finesse.

CHATEAU STE. MICHELLE FUMÉ BLANC (Washington) 1982: Ordered to the table right after the Groth (above), this bottle made a statement in counterpoint to that refined wine. Sappy, fresh, and very grassy, it was delicious and yet less interesting than the Groth. In place of that touch of oak, it had the tang of the grape faithfully rendered. I'd drink it again, too.

ALLEGRO VINEYARD SEYVAL-BLANC (Pennsylvania) 1984: I came across a nearly empty bottle of this wine in the refrigerator of a kitchen in the basement of a Manhattan synagogue where I was doing a stint of voluntary kitchen duty. I have no idea how long the wine had been there. But I do know that it was as cleanly made and crisp a wine as one could want from this grape—a big surprise to me, considering that superior table wine has to be at the bottom of the list of things that Pennsylvania is famous for. This Seyval-Blanc would go perfectly with oysters or fried smelts. It left me wondering which unsung state will next surprise me with a fine American wine.

APPENDIX III
QUICK REFERENCE CHART

GRAPE *Reds*	CHARACTER	BEST FOOD MATCHES	IDEAL AGE AND SERVING TEMPERATURE
Cabernet Sauvignon	firm, often fierce in youth; mellows to interesting nuances like no other red. Black currant and mint are typical flavors of young "Cab." Tobacco, leathery scents come with age.	*The* food wine; a noble partner to lamb, roast chicken or duck, and authentic, crumbly Parmesan cheese. (Not at its best, somehow, with beef.)	best examples need time to round out and deliver full flavor. Age 5–10 is optimum. Serve at 65°.
Pinot Noir	fuller and softer than "Cab"; cherrylike taste in youth, often. Color not so deep as other great reds. "Violets" in the nose.	brings out the best in roast beef and veal; also duck and goose. Adds a voluptuous dimension to mushroom and cream sauces.	young examples can seem rather light. At age 4–8, they should have deepened. Serve at 60°.
Zinfandel	the spicy red, mixing the scent and taste of raspberries, blackberries, and fresh black pepper.	gives a flavor kick to roast turkey; will match up to "spicy" foods and fruit sauces (duck à l'orange) which defeat other wines.	can develop sedate harmony with advanced age. Better to savor its spiciness at age 3–6 years. Serve at 65°.
Merlot	like "Cab," but fleshier and softer. Can seem almost "sweet."	gets along with all dishes that call for red wine—stews most of all	ready sooner than "Cab"—3–5 years. But loses nothing with more aging.
Petite-Syrah	darkest in color, strongest in flavor among reds. But force tends to substitute for subtler facets in its character.	powers its way to an equal standing with char-broiled steak.	softens but doesn't improve with age. Five years is about right.

GRAPE Whites	CHARACTER	BEST FOOD MATCHES	IDEAL AGE AND SERVING TEMPERATURE
Chardonnay	at its American best, you'll keep looking into your glass and wondering where all that intriguing flavor is coming from. Full, dry and deep.	fuller, oak-aged versions ennoble all poultry, rich-fleshed fish like salmon and swordfish. Tops with lobster. Lighter versions with other non-oily fish (flounder, red snapper, trout, etc.).	"Chard" is the only white that benefits from as much as five years in bottle. The best are beautiful at ten years. Serve a bit less chilled than other whites: 55° when young, a touch warmer for old bottles.
Sauvignon Blanc (a.k.a. Fumé Blanc)	firm, vigorous, lively—often with the scent of freshly mown grass. Sometimes blended with the sémillon grape for extra richness.	the ideal "raw bar" white; suits all fish. Has the snap to cut through fried foods such as shrimp and chicken. Does the same to garlicky dishes.	drink young and cold (45°).
Riesling	ranges from dry to ravishingly sweet—but always scintillatingly fruity (you'll most often be reminded of peaches or apricots). Becomes honeyed when very sweet.	shines as a sipping wine—before dinner, even at mid-morning. A gentle partner to delicate fish like trout, cod, flounder, catfish. Nectar-like dessert versions are best sipped alone after dinner is done.	drink young and cold (40°).
Gewürztraminer	a most interesting spicy-floral white. Grind fresh pepper onto a fragrant red rose to get the essence of "Gewürz."	too forceful for most foods except those spiced with ginger or other aggressive flavors. Best sipped alone.	can be sipped young, but a few years in bottle won't hurt. Serve at 45°.
Chenin Blanc	an easy sipper, when off-dry—often hinting at honeydew melon. Less engaging when vinified bone dry.	a perfect summertime aperitif. One of the few wines that gets along well with scallops.	best when young. Serve at 40°.

MISC. WINES	CHARACTER	BEST FOOD MATCHES	IDEAL AGE AND SERVING TEMPERATURE
White Zinfandel (and other "blush" wines)	drinking, not thinking. The best "blush Zins" have verve and even a touch of spiciness.	a wine for lazy days and cook-outs: hot dogs, hamburgers, fried chicken, cold cuts.	must be young. Put it in the ice chest with the beer.
Granache Rosé	the most full-flavored and vibrant of rosés; a touch of sweetness brings out its best.	another picnic wine par excellence. But can be a lively foil to almost any pasta. Lovely with cold lamb.	young and cold (40°).
Sparkling Wine	whether yeasty dry or candy-fruited sweet, "bubbly" is for celebration rather than contemplation.	beyond the happy toasts, think of dry sparkling wine as an adept partner to salty foods—smoked salmon, country ham, even popcorn. It makes a pleasing contrast to creamy soups.	the ceremonial aspects of serving a sparkler shouldn't be ignored. If possible, use champagne "flutes" and keep the bottle in a handsome ice bucket. Serve very cold.
Port (also late-harvest Zinfandel, Essencia, and Elysium)	these sweet, powerfully alcoholic reds are best after dinner or on a cold, rainy afternoon; their flavor is lingering and warming.	stands up to strong cheeses (gorgonzola, cheddar, very ripe brie). Marries well, too, to a nut torte or pound cake. Best of all, sip it alone and oh so slowly.	the older the better. Serve at cool room temperature.

INDEX

ABOUT THE AUTHOR

PETER HELLMAN is a journalist whose work appears regularly in *New York*, *Life*, *The Atlantic*, *Discover*, and *The New York Times*. By avocation he is an expert on wines and good food, and his articles on the subject have appeared in such magazines as *Food and Wine*, *Esquire*, and *Metropolitan Home*. He lives in New York City with his wife, Susan, and his son and daughter.